INDIAN AMERICA
The Black Hawk War

INDIAN
AMERICA
The Black Hawk War

by Miriam Gurko

ILLUSTRATED BY RICHARD CUFFARI

Thomas Y. Crowell Company   *New York*

To Dr. Sidney R. Arbeit,
best of physicians and warmest of friends—
with gratitude and affection.

By the Author:

Clarence Darrow
Indian America: The Black Hawk War
The Lives and Times of Peter Cooper
Restless Spirit: The Life of Edna St. Vincent Millay

Contents

Introduction

The Black Hawk War was a minor episode in the history of the United States. The Sac and Fox tribes who fought in it were not in any way remarkable. They did not have the superior social organization of the Iroquois or the adaptability and progressiveness of the Creeks and Cherokees. Their struggle against the United States lasted only fifteen weeks and could hardly be called a war. But on its own small scale it was typical of all the sad little wars fought on the frontier. It contained all the elements that illustrate the whole tragic story of Indian-white relations. There were the usual misunderstandings between Indians and whites, the badly executed treaties, the broken promises, the betrayals, the split

between the hawks and doves—both white and Indian—
the sufferings of the innocent, the useless heroism, the un-
quenchable land greed which lay at the bottom of it all, and
the agony of being uprooted from long-established homes.
There was the whole rhythm of Indian-frontier movement:
two steps forward, one step back, with the whites always
winning the extra step forward to the West.

Step by step the Indians were forced back by the overwhelming push of the white settlers, but not without violent
resistance in defense of their country. Even after the immense superiority of white military power had convinced
most Indians that resistance was useless, there remained
some whose bitterness and pride led them to one last futile
attempt at keeping their beloved villages. Black Hawk, the
Sac war chief, was one of these, and it is his story that is told
here.

. . . how different is our situation now, from what it was in those days! Then we were as happy as the buffalo on the plains—but now, we are as miserable as the hungry, howling wolf in the prairie!

—from the *Autobiography of Black Hawk*

part one

INDIAN
AND EUROPEAN

chapter one

The Great Discovery

In the eyes of the Europeans, the discovery and conquest of America was a glorious achievement. They had dared to sail beyond the known boundaries of the world, faced the dangers of exploring an unknown land, and survived the enormous hardships of creating a new civilization in a wild and primitive country.

But how did this same exploit look to the Indians already living in that country? After all, they had discovered the same continent thousands of years before, had long since explored it, and had settled it with hundreds of well-defined nations, each with an established culture and tradition. History, like beauty, can rest in the eye of the beholder: even the simplest fact looks very different to someone on the other side of the historical arena. What appeared to European adventurers as one of the world's great triumphs was to the Indians an invasion, ending in disaster.

The Europeans saw America as the New World, land of fresh beginnings. But to the land's first inhabitants, displaced by the irresistible push of the invader or exterminated by his weapons and diseases, it was a world about to end.

For the Indians, too, America had once been a New World. Their old world had been Asia: some ancient disturbance or hunt for food had sent them up through Siberia and into Alaska, not all at once or in any one period of time, but in separate groups over thousands of years. They found an uninhabited continent, settled there, and made it their own. Now after at least fifteen thousand, and perhaps as long as twenty-five thousand years of established ownership, the country was suddenly being taken away from them.

When white men first came from Europe to the Western Hemisphere they found it already occupied by millions of people. It is impossible to know just how many there were, especially since large numbers died soon after the white man arrived, killed off by diseases brought from Europe to which the Indians had no resistance. But there must have been at least thirty million, with perhaps one million in the region that would become the United States. This last group was divided into over six hundred separate nations, speaking almost as many languages and dialects. Some of these languages were as different from each other as English is from Hindustani or Japanese.

Physically, too, the Indians covered a great range: they were every size and shape, with skins that might be anything from reddish bronze to the white of a European. Some had slanted eyes; more did not. Noses were high and arched, or almost flat. The same variations existed in temperament, customs, and ways of living. Tribes like the Apache, Cheyenne, or the members of the Iroquois League had a strong tradition of warfare; others, like the Hopi, Pima, and Papago, disapproved of war, fighting only when absolutely necessary for self-defense. Housing included conical skin tepees, dome-topped wigwams of bark or rushes, log hogans, adobe dwellings, longhouses made of overlapping strips of elm bark, and the amazing "apartment-house" complexes of the Pueblo tribes, rising as high as four or even five stories. Many tribes lived in well-arranged villages, laid out in streets and public squares, with gardens, ball parks, and sometimes fortified walls or palisades.

The country was so vast and fertile, however, that there seemed plenty of room for everyone. The Indians were willing to sell large sections of their territory to the newcomers for ridiculously low prices—an average of three cents an acre during the first three hundred years—and to help them get settled. But in their haste to possess the country, many whites regarded the native as nothing but an obstacle in the way of progress, an object—not quite human in some white eyes—to be brushed aside gently or brutally, depending on one's view of "the Indian problem."

The Indian was not a Christian, nor did he live and think as Europeans did. In the opinion of many Europeans, to be different, especially in religion, was to be inferior. A pagan native was not considered worthy of the same respect and consideration as a fellow European. Some whites wanted to solve the problem of what to do with the Indian by converting him to Christianity and making him over into a copy of the white man. Others proposed to reduce the Indian's land and power until he eventually disappeared. And there were even those who openly advocated direct methods of extermination. Lord Jeffrey Amherst, Governor-General of British North America, considered methods "which may serve to exterminate this accursed race. I should be very glad if . . . hunting them down with dogs were to prove practicable."

Only a small percentage of white men bothered to take a close look at the Indians and see them as real people leading real lives, with customs, religions, and social organizations as valid as those of any other race. And certainly with as much right to their own land as the European trespassers.

For most whites, however, the rapid spread of Christian European civilization over the American continent was seen as progress, something that must not and could not be checked. If the Indians found themselves in the path of such rampaging progress, too bad for the Indians, but it was the divinely sanctioned destiny of white civilization, said these whites, to conquer and transform the country.

What was done to the Indians in the name of this progress was one of the great tragedies of history. Yet much of it might have been avoided with a little patience, some respect on the part of white men for their own laws and treaties, and enough imagination to understand how it all looked to the Indians.

chapter two

The Inconvenient Native

The first contacts were friendly. Explorers and early settlers found the Indians generally hospitable and eager to help. "They are a loving people . . .," wrote Columbus. ". . . they rather invite acceptance of what they possess, and manifest such a generosity that they would give away their own hearts." The settlers of Jamestown, the first successful English colony in America, were able to survive their early hardships only because of the food provided by Powhatan, leader of the Indian confederacy in Virginia. The South was famous for its good cooking and hospitality long before the white man arrived to carry on the tradition.

In Plymouth, the first permanent New England settlement was helped through a similar "starving time" by the

Wampanoag Indians who taught the Pilgrims how to plant corn and dig for clams, and where to catch the best fish. The Pilgrims had never seen corn—Indian maize—and had thought clams were poisonous. Several years earlier Henry Hudson had been welcomed to Manna-Hata, the "hill-island" in the language of the Manhattes Indians, with a feast and ceremonial dances. Perhaps popcorn sweetened with maple sugar, an early Indian delicacy, was served at the feast.

In one newly discovered area after another, these first arrivals were received with friendship and great curiosity. The first vision of men on horses—animals unknown to the Indians—must have been astonishing, something out of their wildest fantasies. The marvelous tools, the bright, keen-edged knives, the soft woven cloth, the unbelievable guns with their startling noise and deadly efficacy, must have appeared like signs of the strongest magic. But the Indians quickly discovered that the miraculous newcomers were men like themselves who could be killed or chased away. Even so, in most instances they treated the white adventurer with the hospitality of hosts entertaining an unexpected guest. "We welcomed him with love," read a sign in the Indian pavilion at Canada's 1967 Exposition. "We sheltered him, we fed him, led him through the forest. . . ."

The white man, however, had some disconcerting ways of responding to this amiability. Columbus kidnapped several of the "loving people" to bring back to Spain, and many later explorers did the same. On his second trip, Columbus sent more than five hundred Indians to Spain to be sold as slaves. The Spanish conquistadors, who soon followed Columbus, took advantage of their friendly reception by enslaving the natives in their own land or reducing them to a state of complete subjection. The devoutly Catholic Spanish did not consider the "heathen" Indians entitled to the same freedom as Christians. Heathens must be converted, by force if necessary, for the good of their souls, or else rooted out. Even converted Indians were ordered to abandon their "excessive liberty" and to work in the mines and fields. Some of the methods used, like cutting off the hands and feet of natives who showed any resistance to Spanish rule, or burning them at the stake, made the much advertised Indian cruelty seem like mild sport by comparison.

The New England Puritans also tried to Christianize the Indian and make him change his habits. They disapproved of his free ways and strange religion, and tried to force him to obey Puritan laws. Killing Indians or selling them into slavery was given the same religious justification among the Puritans as among the Spaniards. During the Pequot War in 1637 most of the tribe, including women and children, were burned inside their village or shot as they tried to escape. Some of the young white soldiers were appalled by the slaughter, but the leaders of Plymouth Colony felt they were doing God's work in destroying unbelievers: "It was as though the finger of God had touched both match and flint." Writing of the event, the sternly devout Increase Mather said, "For the Lord burnt them up in the Fire of his Wrath . . . and it was marvelous in our Eyes." Pequot men who were away from the village were hunted down in the woods and killed, or sold into slavery in the West Indies where the hard labor and unfamiliar climate soon killed them off; their wives and children were distributed among the white victors as slaves.

Almost forty years later, a group of tribes including the powerful Narragansett of Rhode Island, rebelling against the Puritan attempt at domination and land seizure, were cut down in the same way during King Philip's War. The women, children, and old men were slaughtered, their towns and crops burned, and the warriors either tortured to death or enslaved. The wife and ten-year-old son of King Philip, who has been called "the most remarkable of all the Indians of New England," were sold as slaves in Bermuda. Killing Indians and engaging in the slave traffic were not considered sins, especially when such practices were profitable: "Thus the Lord was pleased to smite our enemies and give us their land for an inheritance."

By the end of the seventeenth century, the Wampanoag, Narragansett, Pequot, and Natick, tribes that had welcomed the Pilgrims to New England and without whose assistance they might not have survived, had been almost exterminated by their ungrateful guests. To a descendant of King Philip, this is the way the "Pilgrim Invasion" looked:

December, 1620, the Pilgrims landed at Plymouth, and without asking liberty from any one, they possessed themselves of a portion of the country, and built themselves houses, and then made a treaty, and commanded them [the Indians] to accede to it. This, if now done, would be called an insult and every white man would be called to go out and act the part of a patriot, to defend their country's rights; and if every intruder were butchered, it would be sung upon every hilltop in the Union. . . . And yet the Indians, though many were dissatisfied, without the shedding of blood . . . bore it. And yet for their kindness and resignation towards the whites, they were called savages, and made by God on purpose for them to destroy. . . . The young chiefs . . . were showing the Pilgrims how to live in their country, and find support for their wives and little ones; and for all this, they were receiving the applauses of being savages. The two gentlemen chiefs were Squanto and Samoset, that were so good to the Pilgrims.

In Virginia, too, the English colonists felt that ordinary moral scruples need not be applied in dealing with the natives. When the Indians, alarmed by the rate at which the rapidly increasing settlers were taking over the area, tried to hold back the intruders, war broke out. The colonists forcibly dispossessed the natives and seized their young men and women as slaves. Afterward, when peace terms were being discussed at a treaty council, two hundred and fifty Indian leaders were killed by deliberately poisoned wine. "Wee hold nothinge injust, that may tend to theire ruine" was the explanation.

The enslavement of Indians was not only common during the colonial period, but continued in some parts of the country after the Revolutionary War and lasted even longer than Negro slavery. As late as 1868—five years after the Emancipation Proclamation had freed the Southern Negroes— Apaches were being offered for sale in Arizona for forty dollars apiece, while elsewhere in the West, Navajos were also being sold. Some whites tried to justify the practice on the ground that slavery would serve to "civilize" the Indians by bringing them into close contact with white men's ways.

It never occurred to the white man that the Indian might regard white civilization as inferior to his own. When an Indian refused to accept Christianity or to turn himself into a replica of the white man, his reluctance was put down to stubbornness, stupidity, innate evil, or some mysterious racial shortcoming. Deliberate, outright rejection was the last possible explanation any European would think of.

But it was exactly that. After the first shock of encounter with the white man and his strange and wonderful tools, the Indian with his lively curiosity would carefully observe this remarkable phenomenon. He often made a closer and more thoughtful study of the white man than the other way around. What the Indian saw was a man with less courage and dignity than himself, an ungenerous man with an ignoble passion for money and possessions, and with a corrupt view of land ownership.

The white man, in Indian eyes, would do disgraceful

things for money. He would lie, cheat, demean himself, even risk his life. He would shut himself up all day long inside a dark and airless room or in mines beneath the ground. Or he would spend all his days working under a broiling sun to produce far more than he needed, so that he could sell the surplus for money with which to burden himself with more possessions than he could use. He would even voluntarily give up his freedom and agree to work for another man— just for money.

To the North American Indian, few things were as precious as his personal freedom. There were rare tribal exceptions, like the Natchez of Mississippi, destroyed by the French early in the eighteenth century, with a strong chieftain-dominated society similar to those in Mexico. But practically every other tribe in what is now the United States gave its members a high degree of individual freedom.

The idea of working for another man, or wasting one's days in dull, meaningless labor, was abhorrent. The natives carried on enough agriculture for their own needs, with perhaps a small surplus for trading, but to work excessively just for gain seemed a violation of the basic principles of Indian life. The Indian might freeze, go hungry, suffer acute pain or discomfort, but it never mattered so long as he felt himself free to do whatever he wanted whenever he wanted to do it. Although he trained himself to a rigorous self-discipline, it had to be his own rules or at most those of respected tribal tradition that he followed. When individual tribesmen disagreed about any course of action, one did not try to force his way upon the other. Instead long discussions were held until some mutually acceptable decision was reached, sometimes with the help of the tribal council.

The arts of oratory and debate were highly esteemed and much practiced. Indians could sit for hours and days, listening to each other talk. No one interrupted a speaker, and the natives were shocked at the white man's rudeness in this respect. Eloquence was as greatly respected as bravery, and some of the great chiefs, like Pontiac and Tecumseh, were as renowned for their skill in speechmaking as for their military or political astuteness. White men, in the Indian view, lacked the precious ability to enjoy life. They spent most of their time working, instead of in the pleasurable pursuits of hunting, fishing, playing games, talking with friends and relatives, or enjoying nature. Indians loved games—racing, gambling, archery, playing ball, guessing games—and took delight in social activity of all kinds. There was a great deal of visiting, dancing, singing, joking, story swapping. Far from being the stolid, grim-faced man of legend, the Indian was actually quick to laugh and enjoyed nothing more than a good joke, even a practical joke against himself.

Social organization and behavior varied greatly from tribe to tribe, but all Indians, even those who prized their personal independence most highly, were group people. They played, danced, hunted, planted and harvested crops, performed religious ceremonials, and owned land together, in units ranging from the family to the whole tribe. No Indian had to be alone unless he wanted to be, and he regarded the loneliness and the competitive, self-centered concern of white life as serious drawbacks of that civilization.

As group people, thinking in terms of "we" rather than "I," the Indians felt an abiding responsibility for each other's welfare. They were shocked by white treatment of old people and orphans. The old were deeply respected and played an important part in tribal life; orphaned children were adopted into another family, who loved and cared for them as for their own. Old people took an active role in the education of children, a much more organized process than whites realized. Children were carefully trained in woodcraft; boys were put through rigorous practice sessions in the arts of hunting and warfare. Since there were no written languages and no history books, Indian children memorized the history and legends of their people. Grandparents and other elders of the tribe were often the transmitters of these oral traditions and of religious beliefs and social customs. Children were treated with great affection and kindness. The Indians were astonished to learn that white parents struck their own children, and considered this a form of inexcusable cruelty.

There were no tribal jails or poorhouses. An Indian might be, and often was, hotheaded or temperamental, but he would not steal from or deliberately inflict injury upon his own tribesmen. Anyone unable to feed, clothe, or house himself would be helped by others in the tribe. Indians, generous and hospitable by nature and training, were surprised at the white man's frequent refusal to share his food and possessions freely with those less fortunate than himself.

Another defect of white civilization in Indian eyes was its lack of a close relationship with nature. The Indian loved nature and felt a special kinship with it. Forests, lakes, clouds, trees, all natural phenomena, were living things with which he was in constant and intimate communication, as he was with animals. As one white town after another went up, he was dismayed to see the grass replaced by brick, the trees chopped down, and the game killed or driven off.

Many towns seemed dirty to the Indians. Those who visited England—Europeans were fascinated by Indian visitors and made a great fuss over them—complained about the effect of the soot on their light buckskins. Pocahontas, living in London after her marriage to the Englishman John Rolfe, was troubled by the awful smell of the dirty city. This was a common complaint. There were quite a few tribes with higher standards of cleanliness than the average European of the colonial period. The bathing practices of some tribes struck the Europeans as so extreme that Queen Isabella, issuing orders for Indians under Spanish rule, declared: "They are not to bathe as frequently as hitherto, as we are informed that it does them much harm."

The Indian's religion was closely bound up with nature and was part of his everyday life, as it rarely was with the white men he saw. The Indian was deeply devout and was shocked at the blaspheming of so many white Christians. Though some of the North American natives accepted Christianity, most of them were confused or put off by its contradictions. It preached love and peace, but practiced intolerance and aggression. Above all, Christianity, "the one true religion," the religion of peace and love, was split into hostile camps of Catholic and Protestant, with the Protestants still further divided into quarreling sects.

Chief Spotted Tail, one of the first Sioux to advise his people to accept the white man's way of life, said: "I am bothered what to believe." A "good man" had talked him out of his old faith: "Thinking that he must know more of these matters than an ignorant Indian, I joined his church and became a Methodist." But then the "good man" left, and another came and talked. "I became a Baptist; then another came and talked, and I became a Presbyterian. Now another one has come, and wants me to be an Episcopalian. All these people tell different stories, and each wants me to believe that his special way is the only way to be good and save my soul. I have about made up my mind that either they all lie or that they don't know any more about it than I did at first. I have always believed in the Great Spirit, and worshipped him in my own way. These people don't seem to want to change my belief in the Great Spirit, but to change my way of talking to him. White men have education and books, and ought to know exactly what to do, but hardly any two of them agree on what should be done."

Even if Christianity were free from puzzling contradictions or complicated dogma, it would still have been regarded as a religion shaped by the white man's experience and character, and therefore unsuitable for Indians. A Mohawk, replying to an Anglican missionary who was trying to win converts among his tribe, said: "You Christians were so wicked as to crucify your God, and now he is angry with you, and therefore, to pacify him, you endeavor to persuade us to serve him, but why would we? We never heard of him till Christians came here. He is not angry with us. We never did him any hurt."

Above all, Indians could not understand the land greed of the white man. To the Indians, the earth was a precious gift from the Great Spirit, to be used by all living things and for the good of all. Certain areas might be assigned for the particular use of one group. No Indian would move in on ground containing the home of another or hunt on another's land without permission, but no individual could actually "own" a part of the universal earth. When tribes signed treaties with the whites, they thought they were giving permission to *use* the land, not giving away the land itself for personal ownership, so that no one else could set foot on it.

The Indians watched with astonishment as white men cheated or even killed for a piece of ground. With plenty available for all, why did the whites insist on having it exclusively for themselves? And why, having made an agreement about land, either by treaty or purchase, did the whites break their word and start violating the agreement almost as soon as it was signed? The bad faith and broken promises on the part of white men in matters concerning land were chiefly responsible for the Indians' belief that most whites were liars and cheats, speaking "with a forked tongue," men who could never really be trusted.

Of course, there were some aspects of white civilization that the Indian did admire and hasten to adopt. But these were generally material things: horses, guns, iron tools, copper kettles, steel knives, needles, and chisels. The Cherokee and Creek were impressed by the convenience of writing and after Sequoyah, a highly talented Cherokee, devised his Indian alphabet, printed their own newspapers and books. These tribes also adopted white methods of farming, raising livestock, spinning cloth, and building houses and roads. But like the vast majority of natives, they wanted to retain their own culture. They were Indians, happy to be Indians, and saw little in white civilization that would induce them to stop living as Indians.

If anything, it was the other way around. Thousands of whites, particularly among the French, voluntarily went to live with the Indians and were accepted without prejudice or reservation. Thousands of others who were taken captive and then adopted into the tribes refused to leave their Indian families when the opportunity arose. On the other hand, Indian captives taken by whites could not wait to be returned to their own people.

Certainly, Indian life had its own serious faults and disadvantages. Some tribal cultures were marred by superstition, cruelty, and personal habits and discomforts that whites found distasteful. But the question of which culture was more attractive or superior was really beside the point. The white invaders were not required to admire or copy native life. All they had to do was respect its existence and leave it alone. The main question should not have been, How can we make these people become like us? but, How can we share this rich and magnificent country together? Instead the white newcomers looked at the Indians, found them different, and automatically assumed that they were therefore inferior and expendable.

chapter three

The Marvelous Land

Differences in religion and custom, however, were not the primary reasons for white hostility. The real trouble was the land—the marvelously beautiful and fertile land that the white invaders wanted for their own. Every early account tells of the astonished delight aroused by the sight of the magnificent forests, the quiet lakes, the vast stretches of flowering woodland crossed by sweet-water brooks. In spring, the fragrance of blossoming trees and shrubs along the Atlantic seaboard drifted far out to sea, and boats sailing along the coast sometimes passed through clusters of flowers floating in the water.

The country was not only beautiful to look at but abundantly filled with game and food of every kind. There were great herds of buffalo, antelope, and elk; there were vast numbers of turkeys, some weighing as much as seventy pounds. Quail, wild pigeons, and ducks traveled in flights seven miles long; the coastal waters and inland streams held seafood larger than anything seen in Europe: twelve-foot sturgeon, and oysters measuring almost a foot across. Wild grapes grew everywhere, together with cherries, nuts, wild rice, every variety of berry. Moreover, the land itself proved rich for farming. The Indians had cultivated maize or corn, pumpkins, squash, tomatoes, both white and sweet potatoes, peppers, cashew nuts, peanuts, pineapples, avocados, strawberries, lima, kidney, and many other beans, and hundreds of other food plants unknown in Europe before the discovery of America.

The European newcomers could hardly wait to settle in this Eden. No matter how much land they were able to buy or seize from the natives, it was never enough. Treaty after treaty was signed, establishing definite and supposedly permanent boundaries between white and Indian lands. But as soon as one group of whites settled upon the newly acquired acres, another group came pushing from behind them to still newer areas, swarming over forbidden Indian territory. The Indians believed, and were assured, that a treaty was "forever"—"as long as the grass shall grow and the waters run." But in too many cases, "forever" turned out to be less than a generation.

The big question was, To whom did the land belong? Although the Indians had no individual ownership of land in the European sense, each tribe had its own clearly defined territory, with boundaries that were respected by other tribes. Each specific area had been occupied by the same people, sometimes for hundreds or even thousands of years. Their right to the land was as valid in the eyes of the Indians as if the deeds had been filed, white man's fashion, in the local county seat.

Many whites agreed with this point of view and felt that the right way to acquire land in America was to buy it from the natives, with their full agreement. There were millions of acres available that the Indians were willing to sell or cede by treaty for only a few cents an acre, or in many cases, for some of the white man's cloth, pots and pans, knives, tools, and weapons. These products of white civilization were greatly preferred by the natives to their own; as a result, many tribal handicrafts died out altogether. Manufactured goods became a necessity to the Indians. They were pleased with this aspect of the white man's presence—if only it would remain possible to live in peace with him.

To do this would require a rate of white settlement that was slow enough to give the two cultures time to get used to each other and work out their differences. It would call for patience on the part of the whites: they would have to refrain from using their superior weapons—and later on, their superior numbers—to take what they wanted by force. Most of all, they would have to accept the Indians as the true owners of the land.

Many of the European conquerors refused to take this view. They believed that the land belonged to the "discoverer," meaning the European, not the Indian, discoverer; or to the immediate occupier, which meant that any white man could settle upon a patch of ground upon which the native owner did not happen to be standing at the moment. Above all, they believed in the "right of conquest"—the stronger group could seize territory from the weaker one.

And finally, it was argued that white men had the moral right and duty, the God-given destiny, to take possession of the country because they could make better use of it than the native inhabitants. They would use it, said Senator Thomas

Hart Benton, "according to the intentions of the CREATOR." The Indians, explained the supporters of this view, were too few in number and used the land mainly for hunting instead of agriculture or industry. Didn't the Bible instruct mankind to till the soil, to increase and multiply, and replenish the earth and subdue it?

William Henry Harrison, governor of Indiana Territory, asked, "Is one of the fairest portions of the globe to remain in a state of nature, the haunt of a few wretched savages, when it seems destined by the Creator to give support to a large population and to be the seat of civilization, of science, and of true religion?" And a Congressional committee declared that taking land away from Indians was "sanctioned by the moral superiority allowed to the claims of civilized communities over those of savage tribes." It would be altogether wrong, ran the argument, to leave vast stretches of fertile land in the hands of a few Indian hunters. It would be closer to God's will, and also more efficient and profitable, to establish farms and towns on this land.

Even if this were an acceptable doctrine, it could not be generally applied to the Indians. What its advocates overlooked was the fact that most Indians *were* agriculturists, who had developed many foods that the whites had taken over for their own tables. They had cultivated fields, and lived together in their own kind of towns, many with dwellings set out in regular streets, individual garden plots, and central religious and council buildings.

Many whites believed that all Indians were by nature nomads, who regarded farming as an inferior occupation to be performed by women. But there were tribes, like the Pueblo people, where men did all the farming. In other tribes, the reason for assigning agriculture to women was the belief that they were the fertile sex and that the earth would not be fruitful enough if cultivated by men. And the principal nomads, the Plains Indians, developed their wandering way of life mainly because white men brought the horse to this country. There had once been horses, as well as camels, in America, but they had died out thousands of years ago, and nothing like them had been seen by modern Indians until the Spaniards brought them, along with sheep and goats.

At first, Indians were forbidden to own or ride these "mystery dogs," as they called them, but when the Pueblo tribes revolted against the Spaniards between 1680 and 1692, they seized many of the horses. Other animals strayed away from Spanish *rancherias* and formed wild herds. With the excellent pasturage provided by the spreading grasslands of the plains, these horses—called mustangs, from the Spanish word *mesteños,* meaning wild—multiplied rapidly. During the eighteenth century, horses became increasingly available to the Indians, who soon grew expert at riding and breeding them.

For many tribes living on the edge of the Great Plains, a new life began. Before then, they had permanent villages with fields of beans, corn, squash, tobacco, and other domesticated plants. They were good pottery makers as well as fine gardeners. The horse, however, made it possible for them to follow the great buffalo herds that roamed over the central plains. As a result, the Indians abandoned their regular settlements, their gardens, and their pottery, and created a new kind of existence. It flourished for only fifty years before it began to die out, and involved only a small percentage of the whole Indian population. Yet it was this group, popularized by art and fiction, and later by the movies, that came to represent the typical Indian in the eyes of the whites. And it was the image of the Plains Indian that was given as an example of the wasteful use of valuable land, despite the existence of thousands of natives who were leading settled lives, industriously raising food crops, and tending sheep and cattle.

But whatever justification was given—whether it was to develop the land more efficiently, or to civilize and convert the heathen, or to find new markets for the burgeoning European industries—sooner or later, force was applied. The usual pattern of conquest was for the explorers to appear first, then the missionaries, then the traders, then the settlers, and at last, the army.

One way or another, the whites acquired the precious land. The Spanish conquistadors seized it by "right of conquest." Next came the French who, fortunately for the Indians, were less interested in land than in trade. Instead of establishing colonies, like the English and Dutch who followed them, the French confined themselves mainly to exploring the country and setting up the enormously valuable fur trade, which profited the Indians as well as themselves. Since possession of land never became a great issue between the French and the Indians, relations between them were, with a few special exceptions, generally good. The French liked the Indians as people and admired them as hunters and trappers. They respected Indian customs and recognized the dignity of Indian leaders, negotiating with them on an equal basis as they did with the heads of any responsible state. In their dealings with natives, French traders were more honest and generous than those of other nationalities.

French voyageurs—trappers and traders—traveled without fear among the Indians, who responded with equal respect and affection. The French had no racial prejudice. Many voyageurs spent their lives among the Indians, often marrying native women and taking the trouble to learn native languages. Of all the Europeans who came to America, the French had the best understanding of the Indians and the most successful relations with them.

There were a few instances when the French were subjected to Indian hostility and attacks, as with the Natchez and Fox tribes, which brought sharp retaliation from the French. But the most damaging exception to French-Indian amity concerned the powerful Iroquois confederation, spreading out from western New York State. Early in the seventeenth century the great French explorer Champlain established trade relations with the Algonquin and Huron in the St. Lawrence Valley, unaware that these tribes were engaged in a bitter trade war with the rival Iroquois for control of the region. The French trade—and the guns that the tribes received from Champlain—gave the Algonquin-Huron allies a great advantage over the Iroquois, who from then on regarded the French as hereditary enemies. This had serious consequences for France and perhaps for the whole course of American history. In the contest between the French and British for control of the continent, particularly in the French and Indian War, the Iroquois sided with the British, enabling them to drive the French out of America.

It was the Dutch, with their purchase of Manhattan Island for twenty-four dollars worth of goods, who began the practice of buying land from the Indians. Among the English, men like Roger Williams in Rhode Island and William Penn and his Quaker followers in Pennsylvania also acknowledged the natives as the true owners and bought from them whatever land was needed.

Other Englishmen, however, behaved quite differently, often engaging the local tribes in war, defeating them, and then claiming the land as the property of the British crown. After a treaty was signed, individual Englishmen kept drifting into territory that the Indians had been permitted to keep for themselves. This created more conflict: the Indians would try to drive the intruders off their land, and the intruders would fight back. Eventually men on both sides would be killed, the friends or tribesmen of the slain would seek revenge, and a new incident, perhaps leading to a new war, would be set off. The fact that the trouble had been started by whites trespassing illegally upon treaty-established tribal land was easily brushed aside by the white community.

Neither side took the trouble to discriminate between individual members of the opposite race. If an Indian killed a white, the friends of the white man would regard all Indians as guilty and would kill any native they ran into, though he might be a member of a friendly tribe having nothing to do with the original trouble. The Indians reacted in much the same way: if one white man lied to them or broke a treaty, then all white men were assumed to be treacherous liars. The situation became increasingly tense as more and more land-hungry Englishmen swarmed into the country, and the wall of bitterness and misunderstanding mounted between the two races.

chapter four

France and England

As though white against Indian did not cause enough trouble, another ingredient was added: the conflict between white and white. Almost from the beginning, the European colonial powers competed for control of the new continent; and from the beginning, the Indians were used as pawns in the struggle. Whatever the outcome, the Indians always emerged as the biggest losers.

The whites fought over the Indian trade as well as over the land. They wanted the valuable furs trapped by the natives, and they needed the huge new Indian market for the goods produced in Europe. The English fought the Dutch and Spanish; the Spanish fought the French; above all, the

French fought the English. In the eighteenth century, the rivalry between England and France reached a climax. Each nation tried to stir up the Indians against the other, paying generously for white scalps and prisoners. The French urged the tribes along the frontier, especially in New England, to attack British settlers, often joining in the attack themselves. Bands of French soldiers and Indian warriors, commanded by French officers, would swoop down on exposed towns, with the Frenchmen leading the way in burning and scalping. In Massachusetts the infamous Deerfield massacre was led by the French officer Hertel de Rouville.

European soldiers urged the Indians to use every form of violence against the enemy, at times astonishing the tribesmen with their bloodthirstiness. The Dutch governor of New Amsterdam is said to have started the practice of offering bounties for scalps, Indian scalps in this case, and a similar offer was made at one time or another by most of the later colonial governors. Some commentators even suggest that scalping was introduced by white soldiers and that it was not very different from the English practice of cutting off the ears of poachers. Francis Parkman, the great historian of the last century, no friend of the Indian himself, wrote about the natives and their French associates: "Their fiercest warriors might learn a lesson in ferocity from these heralds of civilization." In the Cherry Valley massacre in New York, it was British officers who killed their white enemies with unspeakable savagery.

When the French first came down from Canada to the Ohio River region, the native inhabitants, already deeply troubled by the English threat, were fearful that these new arrivals would complete the destruction of the Indians. One of their chiefs said to an Englishman: "You and the French are like two edges of a pair of shears, and we are the cloth which is cut to pieces between them." But the French delib-

erately set out to win over the Indians, who came to feel that
they were better off because of the presence of the French.
They never trespassed on Indian lands; were honest and
generous in trading, unlike the notoriously unscrupulous
English traders; and never treated the Indians as inferiors as
so many English had done. The French accepted the native
for what he was, without trying to make him over. When the
French-English rivalry came to its climax with the French
and Indian War, which broke out in 1754, most Indians became allies of the French. The English, like the French, tried
to enlist various tribes to fight on their side or at least remain
neutral, but with the exception of the Iroquois, most tribes
naturally preferred the French.

To win the natives away from the French, the British government recognized the need for a new Indian policy. Steps
were taken, though slowly and at first ineffectually, to do
away with the worst abuses of Indian rights. Under the new
policy, trade and the sale of native land would be regulated
by the government to ensure fair treatment to the Indians,
and settlers would be prevented from trespassing on Indian
lands. A superintendent of Indian affairs for the northern
region and one for the southern were to be appointed to handle complaints, conflicts, and Indian problems in general.

While the new policy was being worked out, however, and
before the Indians could profit by it, the French and Indian
War ended in victory for the English. All of Canada and the
vast eastern section of the Louisiana territory was transferred from French to British control, to the dismay of the
Indians. Till now, they not only had received better treatment from the French but, with two rival countries in the
arena, had been able to play one off against the other. Only
the threat of having the Indians turn to the French had
caused Britain to try to improve her own relations with the

natives. With French competition removed, the Indians feared there would be nothing to check the arrogance of the English, a fear that was reinforced by the blunders of General Amherst, newly appointed commander in chief of all the British forces in North America.

Amherst despised Indians, considering them an inferior race. He had no understanding of them and even less patience, and took exactly those measures guaranteed to antagonize them. He opposed the custom of giving them gifts, a practice that the French had generously observed. With gifts of guns, clothing, and food, the French had won the friendship of even the wildest tribes, and had been able to control vast areas with only a few men stationed in small military and trading posts. Under Amherst, the gifts were either sharply reduced or discontinued altogether. In some cases where gifts were sent, corrupt British agents sold the items to the Indians for high prices instead, keeping the payment for themselves. Such abuses had not occurred under the carefully supervised French administration.

When Indians came to posts formerly held by the French, who had always welcomed their visitors warmly, the new English occupants treated them with contempt and even brutality. English fur traders were also a sorry replacement for the French. The English traders were rough, violent men who cheated and robbed the natives, unlike the French who had been under strict government regulation.

For the Indians, then, the departure of the French marked a new low point in their increasingly difficult position. Their original dislike of the British turned into fear and hatred, emotions stirred still further by the French, who retained a lingering hope that some day, aided by the Indians, they would be able to recapture their lost colonial possessions. The French told their former allies that the British were deliberately planning to exterminate the entire Indian race, a proposal that seemed all too true as the tribes began to feel the effects of Amherst's rule.

Faced with this threat, the Indians took what was for them a rare step. They put aside their tribal differences in a desperate attempt to unite against their enemy.

Ever since the white man began to take over the country and to push the natives back with the advancing frontier, Indian leaders had recognized the ultimate disaster facing their people. They would be destroyed as a race or reduced to unbearable subjection unless they resisted. From time to time an Indian leader would urge the tribes to defend their homes against the alien intruder. But though the whites had often been seriously threatened by Indian attacks, in the end the Indians were always defeated.

To begin with, the whites had superior weapons. By the time the Indians had obtained guns for themselves, the whites had superior numbers. Also, the widely divergent tribes had never been able to unite long enough to drive out their common enemy. The Indians were far from being a uniform group. The peaceful Hopi in the Southwest, the warlike Mohawk in the Northeast, the civilized Creek, and the primitive "Digger," were as unlike each other in language, customs, mentality, and general outlook as the Mediterranean Italian is from the Baltic Swede or Finn. In many cases, the tribes were not only different but hostile, and warring tribes often sided with white armies against each other. White leaders made good use of this intertribal enmity and did all they could to increase it, making it harder than ever for Indians to forget their differences and combine against the whites.

Another handicap was the Indian method of waging war. They never fought long, sustained wars as Europeans did. Instead there were quick raids or brief, contained skirmishes, at the end of which everyone considered the affair settled and went home. They fought in the same way against white opponents, winning a surprising number of battles, and were astonished when the defeated whites did not give up but prepared to fight again. And though they were often great military strategists and always fought with immense courage, the Indians had no conception of a trained, disciplined fighting force, such as the whites had. War chiefs were followed only because their warriors respected and admired them, but the following was entirely voluntary. The individualistic warriors fought when and how they wanted to, and if they saw no immediate necessity for continuing to fight, they simply left. Unless their leader was eloquent enough to persuade them to remain, by appealing to their honor or courage or by stirring their anger or patriotic concern, there was nothing he could do to keep them in the field. To those tribes with a fighting tradition, war was a sport, an exercise, a proof of courageous manhood; it was not the deadly serious, all-out, long-term affair of the whites, waged less for glory than for gain.

Farsighted Indian leaders knew they could never push the whites completely off their land and into the sea, as their followers often believed. But they did hope that by attacking the frontier they could discourage new settlements, and by showing military strength could put themselves in a better position to negotiate with the white treaty makers. At the very least, it might gain them the time needed for the two races to work out a way of living together that would not be ruinous for the Indians. After the French and Indian War, their principal goal was to help restore the French with whom the Indians could survive as equals and who would once again counterbalance the hated British.

The leader who arose after the defeat of the French was

the celebrated Pontiac, a member of the Ottawa tribe. He was a supremely gifted orator, a man of commanding personality and appearance, a political and military chieftain capable of long-range thought and planning. He understood that the only way to resist the whites was for the tribes to forget their differences and work together against the enemy who would otherwise destroy them one at a time. He realized, too, that the threat had become more serious than ever before. Traveling long distances to outlying tribes, he urged the Indians to unite. He succeeded in getting the major Algonquin tribes, together with the Seneca, Mingo, and Wyandot, to join in a sudden and devastating uprising in the spring of 1763. Of the twelve forts in Indian territory, the British could hold only three against Pontiac's onslaught. Amherst now made the statement that seemed to prove the French right when they accused the English of plotting to kill off all the Indians. "Could it not be contrived," he asked, "to send the small pox among the disaffected tribes?"

If Pontiac had been able to keep his followers together, fighting in the manner of white soldiers, he might have driven the British out of Indian territory. But after laying siege to Detroit for six months, his allies grew tired of such extended warfare and began to desert. In the end, with not enough warriors to continue, he accepted the peace terms offered by wiser leaders than Amherst, men who treated him as an honorable enemy. The conclusion of Pontiac's War ended the first large-scale movement toward unified resistance, a step that might have immeasurably lightened the ultimate disaster.

Though Pontiac failed, his unexpected show of strength helped speed the Proclamation of 1763, by which the British government hoped to prevent conflicts, particularly over land, between Indians and colonial settlers. A line was drawn from Canada, along the Appalachian ridge, down to Florida. Everything to the west of the Proclamation Line was reserved for Indians; whites were to remain east of it.

The plan might have worked if the line had been more carefully drawn, if enough money and soldiers had been provided to enforce the ban on white infiltration beyond it, and if some authority had been set up to protect Indians from crimes committed against them on their own side of the barrier. But the Proclamation had been prepared too hastily by a government that was reluctant to send enough money or soldiers to the colonies to defend Indian rights. The greatest obstacle to its success, however, was the impatient rush of the frontier people.

chapter five

The Frontier People

The frontiersman, the wilderness man, the borderer, the
western pioneer, the mover: this was a new kind of American, who lived on the very edge or border of the known
country. He was not an English or Scottish or German colonist, content to find a good piece of farmland and then settle down to cultivate it. He was an American, belonging to a
nation not yet created, giving allegiance to no existing government. He was impatient with traditional ways and authorities, always moving out beyond the established settlements. He could never rest or put down roots as long as there
remained some wild and unexplored territory just over the
next ridge.

In some cases, he was driven not only by his restless search for fresh new space ahead, but by something behind him from which he was trying to escape. It might be the law that he had broken or did not want to obey, or a wife he could no longer abide, or a debt he could not pay, or an enemy whom he feared. It might be just the general pressures and obligations of organized society that he could not accept. In the wilderness there were no dull routines to be followed, no bills, rents, or taxes to pay, no social customs to observe. He could live and dress as he pleased, say what he liked, swear, drink, brawl, carouse, keep whatever hours he wanted, with no disapproving frowns from neighbors or punishment by authority.

The borderers were for the most part rough, coarse, brutal men, "half-horse, half-alligator." Many were misfits who had been unable to get along with other people and had sought the isolation of the frontier. There a man could at last enjoy that complete personal freedom which the Indians knew. The country was magnificent, the hunting and fishing superb, and when he climbed to the crest of that next ridge, he could look down on the vast unpopulated panorama and feel that it was all there just for his own particular pleasure.

Unpopulated, that is, except for Indians who bitterly disputed the borderer's claim that the land was there for him to take. To an Indian a frontiersman was an invader, a trespasser violating the Proclamation Line. The British government, too, considered the westward-pushing American a lawbreaker and took action against him, sending troops to drive him off the forbidden territory, seizing his cattle, even burning his cabin. But so many thousands of illegal squatters poured over the line that the British army and colonial militia, both seriously undermanned, were helpless to restrain more than a fraction of the irresistible horde.

Nor could the government do much about crimes committed by whites against Indians. Distances were too great, authorities too far from the scene of action. Criminals and witnesses could disappear too easily. Even if a case did come to trial, no local jury would find a white man guilty of a crime against an Indian. Murder, theft, illicit trade practices of every kind, went largely unpunished and unchecked.

The Indians made formal protests to colonial governors, army leaders, and the superintendents of Indian affairs. Some Southern colonial governors more or less quietly ignored illegal crossings of the Proclamation Line, because the new settlements strengthened the states' claims to western areas. Many of the Indian complaints, however, were taken seriously and action promised. But as time went on and little was done, as cabin after cabin went up in the wilderness, each placed farther west, the Indians took matters into their own hands. They swooped down upon the illegal frontier people and tried to drive them off by sheer terror, using traditional Indian methods of burning, killing, scalping, and kidnapping. Frontiersmen struck back with equal violence, killing Indians wherever they found them. Many peaceful tribesmen, including groups that had been converted to Christianity, were ruthlessly murdered by whites who refused to recognize any distinction between one Indian and another. They went on Indian-hunting expeditions, shooting them almost for sport. "With the same unconcern," reported an English traveler, "as of killing a deer or a turkey; and with a savage exultation they would mimic him in his dying agonies; and I would venture to pronounce that it would be impossible to find a jury in the back parts of America, who would bring anyone in guilty of murder, for causing the death of an Indian." Such actions, of course, inflamed the border Indians still more, and a period of bloody, relentless warfare set in, carrying with it a bitter interracial hatred.

To the whites, the Indians became "varmints," verminous

obstacles to be wiped out by any means at all. To the Indians, the whites were treacherous intruders, men of no honor, who were stealing the Indian homeland in spite of the British king's assurance that the tribes would be permitted to live there in peace and security.

The families of the wilderness men became as tough and callous as the men. Women joined in the warfare against the natives, and children grew up with an inbred hatred of Indians, learning how to shoot and kill and scalp as a matter of course. Many tribes had frightful methods of torturing their victims, but the frontier people committed the same atrocities with less provocation. The notorious Paxton Boys, a group of brawling young frontiersmen on the Pennsylvania border, broke into the refuge provided for the harmless Conestoga Indians. Defying local authorities who were trying to protect this last remnant of a peaceful tribe, the Paxtons butchered and mutilated the Indians in a fashion that outraged even those eastern whites who had no particular concern for natives. There were other incidents of this kind, arousing the horror of many whites, as well as the fury of the Indians on the border.

Naturally, not all the frontier people were swaggering bullies who spent their time roistering or killing Indians for sport. There were a great many who were neither outcasts nor social misfits, but who had moved west in search of better lives for themselves and their children. There were great woodsmen like Daniel Boone and Simon Kenton, drawn by the magnificence of the country or by a spirit of adventure or even romance. These were the pioneers who embodied the best of the frontier qualities that were to become part of the American national character. They were self-reliant, flexible, optimistic, highly courageous in the face of formidable dangers, and with a sense of values based on individual ability rather than on inherited wealth or position. They created an open society, more progressive and democratic in many ways than could be found on the Eastern Seaboard, where European customs and viewpoints had carried over from the original settlers.

Yet even these men, decent and honest enough as individuals, were determined to occupy the western regions, regardless of the Indians. They tried to deal fairly with the natives, and occasionally formed close friendships with them. But they refused to be driven out. They had fallen in love with the country and were going to hold it and if possible get more of it, even at the risk—and at the Indians' risk—of someone dying in the process.

A curious triangle developed. The frontiersmen hated the government, which tried to force them back of the Proclamation Line, as much as they hated the Indians, regarding them equally as enemies. The government and the settled, law-abiding colonists living along the Eastern Seaboard had their own complaints against the Indians, but despised the frontiersmen as lawless troublemakers who outsavaged the savages. The Indians had accepted the authority of the British government, but furiously resented the white men who crossed into their territory. To the Indians of the frontier these lawless border people represented Americans, as distinguished from Englishmen.

As the Revolutionary War approached, the Indians began to feel about the English as they once had about the French. By this time the English had become their protectors, at least in principle, while the Americans had replaced the earlier English as the enemy. However weak and inadequate British defense of the Indians might be, it was still better than being exposed to the mercies of the Americans. The early English official may have had scorn for the Indian; the new frontier American hated him virulently.

The men of the border felt they had much to gain with independence. They were not in the least concerned with the economic or political motives of the rest of the country. Taxes on tea did not bother them, since they rarely drank it. Taxation without representation bothered them even less, since they had no representation even in the colonial assemblies and never paid taxes anyway. What they wanted was free access to the rich western territories. They believed that if they got rid of the British, the laws preventing them from crossing the Proclamation Line would be canceled. They would also get rid of the British army, which persisted in trying to protect Indians against white squatters. The frontiersmen wanted an American army that would take their side against the Indians instead of the other way around. More than that, they wanted to take control of the country themselves and drive out or kill off all the Indians.

The Indians in turn had everything to lose if America became independent. When the Revolutionary War broke out, most of the tribes sided with the British, despite efforts of American leaders to keep them neutral. Once again, as in the French and Indian War, the Indians found themselves backing the losing side and, as losers, were to suffer new misfortunes.

chapter six

The New Nation

During the Revolutionary War, the English and Americans competed for Indian support. The English gave generous gifts to native leaders and provided the best trade goods at the lowest prices, while paying the highest prices for furs. They warned the Indians that the belligerent Americans were out to steal what was left of tribal lands. American leaders knew it would be impossible to win the Indians as allies after all the frontier trouble, but hoped at least to keep them neutral. Agents were sent out by the Continental Congress to urge the tribes to remain on the sidelines: "This is a family quarrel between us and Old England," they said. "You Indians are not concerned in it. . . . We desire you to remain at home, and not join either side." But most of the Indians, after their painful experiences with land-hungry Americans, felt their only hope of survival lay in helping the British put down this uprising. American independence would surely menace their very existence.

A few chiefs did try to keep their followers neutral. Cornstalk, head of the powerful Shawnee nation and one of the most admired Indians of the period, had tried for years to establish peace between his people and the whites. Determined to keep the Shawnee out of the war, he voluntarily went to the Americans at Fort Randolph to declare his neutrality. The commanding officer seized him as a hostage. While he was being held, Cornstalk, his son, and two accompanying tribesmen were murdered by the garrison's frontier militiamen. Two other native leaders, Big Bullet of the Cherokee and White Eyes, the Delaware chief who had always worked for peaceful relations with the whites, were assassinated on similar peace missions at about the same time. American authorities, greatly embarrassed by these flagrant violations of the rules of safe conduct, tried to smooth things over, even bringing four of Cornstalk's murderers to trial. But no one would testify against them, and the case was dismissed for lack of evidence. The enraged tribesmen gave up all thoughts of neutrality and went over to the British.

Like the French before them, the British encouraged their native allies to use every kind of terror against their white opponents. Indian troops were led by British officers whose savagery shocked even the natives. Henry Hamilton, the British lieutenant governor stationed at Detroit, paid the Indians well for American scalps—he was called the "Hairbuyer." American militiamen retaliated with equal ferocity. They killed Indian women and children, and scalped and mutilated with none of the revulsion that white men were supposed to feel at such actions. Many state assemblies offered generous bounties for each warrior's scalp turned in, with smaller payments for those of Indian women and children. A militiaman, reproved for killing a native child, calmly replied, "Nits make lice."

Indians who remained neutral were slaughtered along with the rest. Ninety peaceful, unarmed mission Indians in Ohio, converted to Christianity by the Moravians, were herded into their chapel and threatened with death. They asked for a few hours delay in order to prepare themselves. It was granted, and after a night of prayer and hymn singing, they were clubbed to death and then scalped by the trophy-collecting militiamen.

Every outrage committed by border militiamen produced a new series of violent Indian counterattacks. Settlements and outlying cabins were burned, and the inhabitants murdered or taken prisoner. Captured American soldiers were tortured with special brutality. Long after the war was over, each side retained anguished and unforgiving memories of the terror and cruelties inflicted by the other. Peaceful coexistence seemed impossible. When the war ended in victory for the Americans, a cry went up for the seizure of all Indian territory. The Indians, as British allies, were defeated enemies, ran the argument, and so had forfeited their right to the land. It should be thrown open to white settlement. The peace treaty, signed by the British without consulting their native allies, made no provision for the protection of Indian land rights. Deserted by their English friends, the Indians had to face the belligerent Americans alone.

The new American government, however, rejected the demand for seizing native territory and accepted the same responsibility for the welfare of the Indians that the British had assumed. Men like Jefferson, Washington, and Henry Knox, first Secretary of War and in charge of Indian affairs, acknowledged the right of the tribes to live unmolested on their own land. Jefferson said: ". . . not a foot of land will ever be taken from the Indians without their consent. The sacredness of their rights is felt by all thinking persons in America as much as in Europe." These men also recognized the danger of continued border warfare if the Indians' need for a place to live was disregarded.

But faced with the monumental problems of creating a new country, the United States was even less able than Britain to carry out its good intentions. The pressures from frontiersmen and newly organized land companies were too great for the insecure young government to ignore. Some Southern states seized Indian territory and threatened to break away from the still untried Union if Congress interfered.

The Federal government established an Indian Department and enacted laws to protect the Indians; but it lacked the power to enforce the laws, so not much protecting was done. The Northwest Territory Ordinance specifically stated: "The utmost good faith shall always be observed towards the Indians, their lands and property shall never be taken from them without their consent; and in their property, rights, and liberty, they never shall be invaded or disturbed, unless in just and lawful wars authorized by Congress. . . ." But frontiersmen continued to invade and disturb the Indians and the Federal government could do little about it. The army was occasionally sent out to punish and remove the invaders but officers were instructed to treat white squatters "with all the humanity" possible. In effect, this meant that if white and Indian interests clashed, the army would protect the whites.

As thousands of pioneers swept into Kentucky and along the Ohio River with scarcely a check from the new government, the Indians became increasingly alarmed and continued to harass the newcomers, hoping to scare them off. The frontier people continued to fight back. Border incidents flared into military engagements, with the militia or army coming in to restore order. Peace may have come to the Eastern Seaboard with the end of the Revolution, but on the frontier, war raged as violently as ever.

The Indians felt they were making their last stand for survival. In this time of crisis, several great native leaders came forward. One of these was Joseph Brant, the remarkable Mohawk who had spent his life as much in the white as in the native world, and considered himself as much an Englishman as an Indian. He had received an excellent education and spoke and wrote English fluently; he became converted to Christianity and gave a good deal of help to missionaries working among the Iroquois tribes. On his visits to London, he was entertained at the royal palace. Many prominent Englishmen, including James Boswell and the Prince of Wales, became his friends. He could easily have remained in the white man's world, but his chief concern was for the Indians. He spent most of his life trying to help his people survive the onslaught of white civilization.

Because of his travels in America and Europe he understood, as few other Indians did, the immense size and power of the white race. He knew that the most sustained or effective border raids could not possibly hold back the surge of white settlement. The only hope for the Indians, he felt, was to develop their skills as farmers, as sheep and cattle breeders, or as artisans.

During the Revolution he and his Iroquois followers fought for the British in exchange for their promise to protect the Indians, to provide them with the time and living space they needed before they could adapt themselves to the new circumstances of white civilization. When England lost the war, Brant was faced with the problem of winning the necessary respite from the vengeful, impatient Americans.

He came to the same conclusion that Pontiac had reached twenty years before. The only solution was for all the tribes to unite in one powerful confederation. Individual tribes did not have enough strength to face the Americans. One by one, either through wars or by forced treaties, the tribes would be deprived of their lands and turned into homeless wanderers. Acting together, they might command enough respect to work out a tolerable arrangement with the American government. Or, failing peaceful negotiation, they might be strong enough—especially with the British military help Brant hoped to get—to cause enough trouble so that the Americans might agree to satisfactory truce terms. In either case, all-Indian unity might provide some kind of bargaining position. Without unity they would lose everything.

Brant worked in every possible way to create an effective Indian confederation, but like Pontiac before him, he was defeated in the end by his own people. Despite all they had been through, the Indians were still temperamentally incapable of forgetting tribal differences or individual convenience long enough to sustain their common struggle. Inter-tribal jealousies led to distrust. It became impossible for the leaders to agree on what course to follow. At last Brant had to give up his dream of a powerful and united Indian confederation. With a large group of Iroquois he went to live in Canada, while the United States continued to defeat one separate Indian group after another and to push the frontier farther and farther west.

Another great native leader was Tecumseh, the Shawnee chief. Like Brant he could speak, read, and write English fluently, and had read widely in English literature and history. Like both Brant and Pontiac, Tecumseh knew that the only hope for Indian survival lay in Indian unity. He spent years traveling over the country from Florida to the Great

Lakes, urging the tribes to form a confederacy. "The annihilation of our race is at hand," he declared, "unless we unite in one common cause against the common foe." He wanted the Indians to renounce many aspects of white civilization, particularly the use of alcohol, which had an especially disastrous effect upon them, and to refuse to sell land to the whites on an individual tribal basis. The land, he said, was the common heritage of all Indians; no part of it could be disposed of by a single tribe without ultimate harm to all. He urged his people to think of themselves not as Shawnees or Cherokees or Kickapoos or Potawatomies, but as Indians. He dreamed of a separate Indian nation, independent of the United States, living safely and peacefully inside its own permanently defined borders without fear of continued encroachment by the whites.

Tecumseh was a brilliant and impassioned orator, changing the pitch of his voice to suit the mood of the occasion and using dramatic devices to make his points. In one famous council with General William Henry Harrison, Tecumseh asked, "How can we have confidence in the white people? When Jesus Christ came upon the earth, you killed Him, and nailed Him to a cross." Later, during the same council, Harrison paid a visit to Tecumseh's camp. The two leaders, red and white, sat down on a bench. Tecumseh sat very close to Harrison and gently pushed against him. Harrison moved away slightly, but Tecumseh moved with him. He kept pushing in this way until Harrison was at the very end of the bench and protested that he would be pushed off. Tecumseh laughed and said that was exactly what the westward-moving white settlers were doing to the Indians.

He was a skillful organizer, bringing together thousands of warriors from diverse tribes under his leadership. Assisting him in building up an Indian confederacy was his brother Tenskwatawa, known as the Prophet. Harrison recognized the military strength of the Shawnee brothers and resolved to destroy it before they could rally the tribes into a united defense against further invasion by the whites.

In the summer of 1811, Tecumseh left Indiana for a six-month recruiting trip among the tribes of the South. The Prophet remained behind in his village on the Tippecanoe River. Harrison, knowing that Tecumseh was the real military leader of the growing confederacy, decided this would be an opportune time to attack. Early in November, Harrison provoked the braves in the Prophet's town into battle. With an army greatly outnumbering the warriors, he easily drove back the Indians. The town was abandoned, and Harrison ordered it destroyed.

The Battle of Tippecanoe was a relatively small victory, but much was made of it. Its importance was magnified until by 1840 the slogan of "Tippecanoe and Tyler too!" helped win the Presidency for Harrison.

Tecumseh was furious when he learned of the Indian defeat, but it did not stop him. On the contrary, he increased his attempts to urge the Indians into taking defensive action against the Americans. When the War of 1812 broke out, Tecumseh joined the English, hoping for their assistance in holding back the American advance and in setting up his Indian empire. The British would have welcomed an Indian buffer state between Canada and the United States. But once again the Indians backed the wrong group. Like Pontiac, who had hoped to bring back the French, and Brant, who lost with the British in the Revolutionary War, and the Five Civilized Tribes, who would later back the South in the Civil War, Tecumseh found himself on the losing side.

He was killed in the Battle of the Thames, in which the British suffered one of their worst defeats of the war. The day before the battle he had a premonition of his death and gave away his possessions. His tomahawk was given to one of his most devoted allies, Black Hawk, leader of a group of Sac Indians who had supported the British cause.

With Tecumseh's death his confederacy fell apart. Indian power in the Northwest was broken, and the land between the Ohio and Mississippi was left defenseless against white invasion.

A similar rise and fall of Indian resistance took place in the South, particularly among the Creek. Here the struggle was complicated by internal disagreements on how to deal with the new American government. The Creek, like the Cherokee and the other members of the Five Civilized Tribes—Chickasaw, Choctaw, and Seminole—had made the most successful Indian adjustment to white civilization. They had prosperous farms and towns with schools, gristmills, taverns, ferries, a code of laws, and some form of representative government. They had large herds of cattle and fruitful orchards, and raised a great variety of crops, including cotton which they processed and wove into cloth. They wore the white man's style of clothing. Most of the Creeks believed it would be possible to live peacefully with the Americans and rejected Tecumseh's pleas for an armed confederacy.

There were some, however, who listened to Tecumseh. They felt that the whites of Georgia would continue to demand more and more Creek land as they had done in the past, and that a firm stand must be taken against the Americans and against the white customs which the rest of the tribe was adopting. In the War of 1812 this group became allies of the British, against the strong opposition of their fellow tribesmen.

At first the Creek allies of the British were successful in their encounters with the American army, and the United States became alarmed. General Andrew Jackson marched down from Tennessee at the head of an army consisting of state militia and a large number of pro-American Creek, Cherokee, and Choctaw Indians. In the spring of 1814, about six months after the death of Tecumseh in the Battle of the Thames, Jackson with the aid of his Indian allies defeated the Creeks in the equally decisive Battle of Horseshoe Bend.

The peace treaty that Jackson imposed upon the Creeks proved that Tecumseh had been right when he insisted that if Indians did not act as one people in their dealings with the whites, they would all suffer. At the treaty of Fort Jackson, the Indians who had fought on the side of the general were punished equally with those who had opposed him. The entire Creek nation was forced to give up two thirds of its land, chiefly in Alabama and Georgia. Jackson's Cherokee and Choctaw allies would also lose their land later on. By permitting themselves to be divided and assisting in their own defeat, the Indians of the South lost their power forever.

With Indian strength broken in both North and South, the United States could now easily chip away at the land held by separate tribes. It was no longer necessary to fight bloody and expensive wars in order to take over native territory: it could be done by a succession of the most questionable treaties ever imposed by a strong nation upon a weak and inexperienced people.

The Indians were forced, tricked, cajoled, or threatened into signing treaties giving away their land. A common early practice was for Federal agents to seek out a few minor tribal chiefs, particularly weak or corrupt individuals, get them drunk or give them a sum of money or a few gifts, and then have them sign a treaty in the name of the entire tribe. Or the agents would take ordinary tribesmen, "appoint" them chiefs, and then get them to sign. By the time the rest of the tribe heard about it and protested, it would be too late: the Federal agent would produce the treaty and point to the signatures. These were generally no more than marks scrawled on documents that the native signers were unable to read and whose contents they did not fully understand. Sometimes the "signatures" were outright forgeries, written by the agents themselves. But the Federal authorities would insist that the land had been legally transferred and the Indians must move off.

Another favorite technique, recommended by Thomas Jefferson, was to get tribal chiefs in debt to the trading posts that the Federal government was setting up in Indian territory. "We observe," said Jefferson, "that when these debts get beyond what the individuals can pay, they become willing to lop them off by a cession of lands." Since the Indians knew little about white trading practices and even less about the market value of goods, it was common for an exchange of goods to end up with the natives owing money.

As the United States became stronger and the Indians weaker, Federal authorities or army officers would call a conference of Indians and announce that the government needed a portion of their land. The Indians were then given a choice of either signing a treaty voluntarily in exchange for cash or annual payments and gifts or of having the army seize the area by force under less favorable terms. The one choice they did not have was to keep the land for themselves.

All kinds of pretexts were used to get Indians to sign away the land. Tribes had to yield large tracts as punishment for the wrongdoings of only a few of its members—who were not always guilty of the crimes charged against them. Or a tribe would be asked to sign a treaty giving up land at some date in the distant future while retaining the right to use it themselves in the meantime. This was very confusing to most natives, who had only a vague understanding of the white man's real estate laws and customs. Many Indians thought they were selling only the right to use the land, not the ground itself, and were dismayed when they were thrown out of their homes and forbidden all further access to territory their people had lived on for generations. In the case of the "delayed-occupation" treaty, either the Indians were in for a nasty surprise when they were informed that their homes had been sold many years earlier or, as it generally turned out, the land was required by the whites much sooner than expected. Even when the Federal government set a definite date for occupation with every intention of abiding by that date, land speculators or pioneer settlers would be too impatient to wait. They would rush in to occupy the land before the ink on the treaty had a chance to dry.

When this happened, local authorities shrugged their shoulders and did little or nothing to prevent the illegal occupation. Even the agents appointed by the government to protect the Indians often cheated them. A good deal of the money paid by the United States for Indian land found its way into the pockets of these agents instead of being handed over to the tribe.

But the greatest disillusionment of all was the failure of the government in Washington to live up to its own earnest promises. Every treaty offered to the Indians was supposed to be the final one. The remaining land was guaranteed to belong to them forever, "as long as the grass shall grow and the waters run." Yet only a few years after these words had been solemnly inscribed upon a document, the government would demand another treaty yielding more acreage. This time, the authorities would promise, it would really be permanent. But it never was. There was hardly a treaty signed at that time that lasted for even as long as twenty years.

By such means, millions of acres were transferred from

Indian to white ownership. For the whites it meant the opening of vast new areas for settlement, the creation of new territories and new states. The Territory of Indiana was created in 1800, when it contained only twenty-five hundred whites. In the next ten years the population swelled to twenty-five thousand. By 1825 eleven new states had been added to the original thirteen.

To the Indians it meant an alarming shrinkage of living space. Tribes were pushed out of their established homelands and into areas that were already filled with Indians who had been forced to leave the East at some earlier time. Hunting areas grew crowded, and what game was left began to disappear as white settlement moved west. The white man acted upon the Indian, said Henry Adams, like acid: "As the line of American settlements approached, the nearest Indian tribes withered away."

It all happened so swiftly that an Indian might find himself dispossessed and transplanted several times in the course of a few years. Many displaced natives could not adjust to such a succession of uprootings. They grew discouraged, apathetic, or completely demoralized, dependent on government subsidies or white men's handouts. It has been said that they were suffering from a form of culture shock: they had been exposed to white civilization so abruptly, and their lives changed so quickly, that they could not rebound from the stunning effect of it all.

As hunting declined, there was not only less food but less for the warriors to do. A few began to drink heavily. For some reason Indians have always been particularly susceptible to the effects of alcohol. They had known nothing of strong drink until it was introduced by the whites, and many Indians took avidly to this wonderful firewater. Early traders would often get an Indian drunk, then get him to exchange valuable furs for a few trinkets or another jug of whisky.

Vast acreages of land were coaxed away from natives through the same deliberate use of liquor. Leaders like Tecumseh tried to ban alcohol, and many chiefs pleaded with white authorities to forbid the sale of liquor to natives. Such laws were often passed, but there were always white men who found it to their advantage to use liquor in their dealings with Indians, and the laws were easy to evade.

As though in return for alcohol, the Indians gave the white man tobacco, which had been completely unknown in Europe before Columbus came to America. The habit of smoking, as well as chewing and snuffing tobacco, spread immediately and rapidly all over Europe and the rest of the world.

Most Indians, however, took to neither drink nor apathetic despair. They did what they could to accommodate themselves to the new conditions. Some retreated quietly to the West and tried to resume life as before. Others, particularly among the Five Civilized Tribes, took up new occupations and new ways of life, often with remarkable success. But whatever they did, the threat of white land hunger was still there and growing stronger.

An endless number of pioneers kept moving west until the Indians began to feel as though they were drowning in the rapid tide of white settlement. But it was still not fast enough for the settlers who wanted fertile farmland at low prices, the land speculators who wanted quick profits from the sale of new town sites, the miners who wanted free access to Indian lead and gold mines, and the Federal government which needed the money it could get from the sale of new territory acquired from the Indians.

The method of getting land from the Indians piece by piece through treaties now appeared too slow and cumbersome. Why not, asked men like President Andrew Jackson, take all the land at once? Why not expel all the Indians still living east of the Mississippi and resettle them west of the river?

In response to this demand, Congress passed the Indian Removal Act in 1830, clearing the way at last for the almost complete replacement by whites of the original population east of the Mississippi.

chapter seven

Removal: The Trail of Tears

President Andrew Jackson was a westerner, raised on the frontier. He had been a famous Indian fighter, called Sharp Knife or the Pointed Arrow by the tribes, though after his removal policy went into effect, the Cherokees called him the Chicken Snake. Like most frontiersmen he had little use for Indians: he considered them a nuisance and an obstacle to national expansion. The idea of dealing with the tribes as independent nations seemed ridiculous to him: "I have long viewed treaties with the Indians as an absurdity. . . . The Indians are the subjects of the United States, inhabiting its territory and acknowledging its sovereignty. Then is it not absurd for the sovereign to negotiate by treaty with the subject?"

Indians, he claimed, were not even citizens of the United States and therefore not entitled to the same rights as citizens. They were only subjects, and Congress could therefore dispose of their affairs by passing whatever laws it considered desirable, and the Indians would have to obey. To Jackson, the expulsion of all Indians from the area east of the Mississippi River seemed highly desirable and he urged Congress to pass the Removal Act in May 1830. Under its provisions the Indians were to be given land west of the Mississippi in exchange for their lands east of the river. The Federal government would help them move and furnish assistance in establishing new homes.

The Indians were devastated. They had an emotional and religious attachment to their land which few whites were able to understand. Indians felt a special kinship with a particular piece of earth, were part of it. The fact that their ancestors were buried there gave the area a deeper significance and made the prospect of leaving it especially painful. In the past when land was sold to white men, the tribes always tried to retain part of the original territory for their own use. Or, if forced to give it all up, they had moved back as little as possible, to areas not too unlike their former homes. Now they were being asked to go a long distance to completely foreign territory.

They were fearful about the new wild country. The West contained strange and possibly hostile tribes; the climate and landscape would be vastly different from their beloved eastern woodlands. They would have to give up their fertile fields and established towns and start life over again on the dry western plains—an area then known as the Great American Desert, considered unfit for white men and generally worthless. This was, of course, why it was being handed over to the Indians. As soon as the value of the western plains was recognized, the Indians would again be asked to move, despite the assurance under the Removal Act agreements that they would be allowed to remain in their new homes forever, with no further interference.

Many whites were also appalled by the Removal Act, regarding it as a monstrous injustice. Ralph Waldo Emerson called it abhorrent, and there had been a strong movement to prevent its passage. There were mass meetings and petitions, and bitter debates in Congress. But the supporters of the bill used the old argument that whites could make better and more profitable use of the land. They declared that God had intended the land for white agriculturists rather than Indian hunters. Had not God commanded man to till the earth? This argument conveniently ignored the large percentage of Indians then living east of the Mississippi who were settled farmers. In the South especially, the Five Civilized Tribes had thousands of acres under intensive cultivation, raising the same crops and tending the same herds as their white neighbors.

A final argument was that the Removal Act would be best for the Indians themselves: It would remove them, said Jackson, from the "degradation and destruction" of contact with the white race, and would place them "beyond the reach of injury or oppression." In effect, the Indians must be rescued from civilization.

By this time the Indians living in the eastern part of the United States had been exposed to over two hundred years of civilization. Thousands had adopted the white man's tools, crafts, housing, and clothing, his methods of farming and manufacturing, his systems of education and organized government, even his religion. These were the people who now, at this late day, were going to be saved from white civilization. These were the "nomadic" tribes who had to be removed to make place for the white farmer. These also happened to be the people who owned some of the richest farming land in the East and upon whose territory gold, lead, and other valuable ores were to be found. And finally, these were the people who had never been granted citizenship in the nation that had grown up around them, and so could not vote against the President who asked for the passage of the Removal Act.

Earlier Presidents had considered the possibility of moving the natives west as a solution to "the Indian problem." Some even considered establishing a separate Indian state. Jefferson had planned to set up Louisiana as a reservation for all Indians east of the Mississippi. Many tribes did move, not always voluntarily. Under Jackson, however, removal was organized and carried out on the largest possible scale.

Once the act was passed, Jackson moved quickly. Agents were sent to all the tribes; arrangements were made, and contracts drawn up, sometimes before the bewildered Indians had time to realize just what was happening. The removal agreements generally specified a waiting period of up to several years, to give the government time to find new locations and to allow for gradual preparation, disposal of property, and the details of emigration. But before the stated time, or even before the agreements were ratified, whites began moving into Indian territory, driving off the natives, seizing their crops and livestock, moving into their homes or burning them down, and beating up any Indian who tried to defend his home and property.

When the Indians appealed to the Federal government for protection, Federal officials replied that they had no power to prevent such acts and that it would be best for the Indians to leave as soon as possible. On the rare occasions when Federal marshals tried to save Indian property, local whites put up a strong fight backed by state authorities.

The Indians were supposed to receive a fair price for their lands and whatever goods they would have to leave behind, but unscrupulous dealers quickly entered the scene and defrauded them in a variety of ingenious ways. Inexperienced

Indians, unaware in many cases of the real value of their property and under the pressure of frightening events or physical threats, accepted ridiculously low prices or took payment in bank notes that turned out to be worthless. Some whites seized Indian farms and equipment in payment, they claimed, for debts. These debts were generally imaginary or grossly exaggerated, but the Indians were in no position to prove it or to sue for the return of their property, especially since natives were forbidden by law to testify in cases involving a white man. All too often, everything movable was simply stolen outright; even Indian graves were dug up so that silver jewelry and other valuable objects, buried with the dead according to native custom, could be looted.

Among the saddest events was the treatment of the forty thousand Creeks and Cherokees, the most civilized, progressive, and altogether remarkable group of Indians in the South. Far from being wandering hunters who had to be removed to make place for settled farmers, as the advocates of removal claimed, they were permanently established, as devoted to the Biblical injunction to till the soil as any of their white neighbors. They lived in comfortable, well-furnished houses on prosperous farms or in highly organized, well-policed towns of their own. In 1821 Sequoyah had invented an alphabet for the Cherokee language. Within a few years, virtually the whole tribe learned how to read and write, becoming a literate people in less time than any other group in the world's history. Libraries were assembled, with one district boasting of its "1000 good books." In 1828 the *Cherokee Phoenix,* the tribal newspaper, began publication. A written code of laws and a constitution were adopted, establishing trial by jury and encouraging a system of education. The Creek soon took over Sequoyah's alphabet, and the Bible was translated into both languages. A little later, Sequoyah helped develop a written language for the Choctaw.

The lands occupied by these Southern tribes were coveted by white planters, who wanted to extend their cotton empire. The planters were naturally among the warmest supporters of the Removal Act, and regarded Indian removal as Jackson's greatest accomplishment.

The Cherokee and some of the Creeks opposed the first attempts to remove them from their homes. The Cherokee, under their very able leader John Ross, put up a strong legal battle against the state of Georgia, which was trying to force the Indians to give up their land, especially after gold was discovered on it. The tribe asked for the Federal protection to which they were entitled under their treaty with the United States. In a famous test case before the Supreme Court, Chief Justice John Marshall decided in favor of the Cherokee, but President Jackson still refused to protect the Indians. He said: "John Marshall has made his decision. Now let him enforce it." Local authorities continued to harass the Cherokee, but for several years the tribe said firmly that it would not yield its land or its legal rights. Finally, in May 1838, President Martin Van Buren sent General Winfield Scott with seven thousand soldiers, not to protect the Cherokee, but to round them up and take them west.

Only a small number of Creeks resisted, and they were quickly defeated. But as a result the immediate removal of the entire tribe was ordered in 1836. The eviction of both tribes was carried out in surprise attacks. They were forcibly seized—dragged from their homes or taken while working in their fields—with no time to make arrangements for selling their property or even to take anything along with them. They were put on the road to exile without provisions for the journey or the necessary equipment for their new life, without tools, plows, kitchen utensils, spinning wheels, blankets, clothes, and without their horses and wagons in which to transport themselves and their goods. They had to leave in the light summer clothing they were wearing at the time of seizure, and thousands died when the weather turned cold. Local white residents came with the soldiers and, as the Indians were taken out, moved in immediately. Many natives barely got out of a cherished home when they saw it go up in flames or watched their cattle being driven off and their valued possessions carried away by white vandals. Some of the Creeks fled and hid in the surrounding forests. They were hunted down; some of those captured were put into handcuffs and sent to join the rest of the tribe going west; others were executed. Many women and children were handed over to white families as slaves.

The journey west was harrowing, not only for the Creek and Cherokee, but for the rest of the Southern tribes. The Federal government had arranged with private contractors to provide transportation and food, but every kind of cheating took place. The contractors overcharged the government outrageously for supplies or spent a minimum of the allotted funds, pocketing the rest. They bought rotting, inedible food, which made the Indians ill or which was so bad that some tribes refused to eat it and had to go on buffalo hunts along the way to keep themselves alive. When they came to rivers, ancient, unsafe boats were chartered, on which living conditions were appalling. Baggage, left behind to be forwarded later by the contractors, was never sent. The inferior wagons and oxcarts provided by the contractors broke down, with more loss of Indian possessions. Some tribes had been able to take along their livestock, but gangs of horse and cattle thieves followed the exodus. The Indians posted guards at night, but hundreds of animals were stolen just the same.

There was enormous loss of life. Boats were dangerously overloaded and carelessly handled; there were many deaths by drowning as a result. Others died of diseases caused by lack of decent food or adequate clothing and shelter. There

were outbreaks of cholera and measles, with heavy fatalities.
Drenching rains aggravated the illness and turned the roads
into impassable mud. Later there was snow and ice to con-
tend with. Many of the Indians who had worn out their shoes
and were walking barefoot suffered from frostbite. A large
number died from sheer exhaustion and, as the Indians
themselves put it, heartbreak. Four thousand Cherokees—
almost a quarter of the tribe—and half the Creeks died on
or because of the journey. The Cherokee called it the *Ho-de-
no-sau-nee,* the trail of tears.

As the Creeks trudged along, one of the women made up a
song which they all began to sing:

> I have no more land.
> I am driven away from home
> Driven up the red waters
> Let us all go.
> Let us all die together. . . .

The behavior of the regular army soldiers who accompanied the emigration remains one of the few redeeming aspects of the whole shameful episode. They shared their rations with the Indians, nursed them through sickness, and
did what they could to ease their discomfort. White people
living along the line of march were also moved by the tragic
spectacle and sometimes provided food and warm clothing.

One deeply moved spectator was Alexis de Tocqueville, a
young Frenchman who spent almost a year traveling around
the United States and Canada, making a detailed and
thoughtful study of conditions that he later described in his
book *Democracy in America.* He arrived in 1831, just when
removal was taking place. The Indians held a particular interest for him, and he went by steamer, stagecoach, and
horseback to every frontier he could reach. He was in
Memphis, on the east bank of the Mississippi, when the Choc-
taws crossed the river. "It is impossible to conceive the

frightful sufferings that attend these forced migrations," he wrote. "They are undertaken by a people already exhausted and reduced; and the countries to which the newcomers betake themselves are inhabited by other tribes, which receive them with jealous hostility. Hunger is in the rear, war awaits them, and misery besets them on all sides. . . . It was in the middle of winter, and the cold was unusually severe; the snow had frozen hard upon the ground, and the river was drifting huge masses of ice. The Indians had their families with them, and they brought in their train the wounded and the sick, with children newly born and old men upon the verge of death. They possessed neither tents nor wagons, but only their arms and some provisions. I saw them embark to pass the mighty river, and never will that solemn spectacle fade from my remembrance. No cry, no sob, was heard among the assembled crowd; all were silent. Their calamities were of ancient date, and they knew them to be irremediable."

Not all the tribes went through the wretched experiences of the Southern Indians. Some moved with relatively minor trouble. But they all suffered to some degree from the uprooting and transference to the West. Most of them went quietly, if miserably, feeling there was nothing they could do against the power of the United States.

But besides the Cherokee and Creek, two other groups refused to be expelled from their homes that easily and made a last-ditch stand to defend themselves. The Seminole, under Chief Osceola and his successors, retreated into the Florida Everglades where they defied the United States for ten years until the government, having spent almost sixty million dollars trying to subdue them, gave up and allowed them to remain, secluded in the inhospitable swamps. The other group was a small band of Sac and Fox Indians led by the old war chief Black Hawk.

part two

THE WAR

Location of Black Hawk's home territory and of the Black Hawk War

chapter one

Saukenuk

In the northwestern corner of Illinois, where the Rock River joins the Mississippi and where the city of Rock Island is located today, stood the Indian town of Saukenuk. It was an excellent location, on a busy trade route, and Saukenuk was a flourishing place. A whole string of Sac and Fox villages lay along the Mississippi in what are now the states of Wisconsin, Illinois, and Iowa, but Saukenuk, more than a hundred years old and at the very center of the Sac and Fox country, was the largest and most important.

It was a Sac village. The Fox tribe had originally come from another part of the Great Lakes region. In the early eighteenth century, because of trouble with white traders, they were driven out by the French and took refuge with the Sac. From then on the two tribes remained closely allied, and though each had its own villages, they fought and acted as one group. At the end of the eighteenth century there were almost five thousand Sac and sixteen hundred Fox. Physically they were fairly similar: tall, well built, with rather light skins.

The Sac were the leaders of the combined tribes, not only because of their greater numbers, but because they had a superior gift for political organization and were famous throughout the area for their fighting abilities, their great courage, and their high spirit. They were a proud, fiercely independent people, with a strong sense of personal dignity. The Fox were also brave and warlike, but less skilled politically. They were content to follow the capable Sac chiefs.

Saukenuk was an unusually pleasant, well-cared-for town. It was laid out in regular streets with a central square and surrounded by a palisade with entrance gates. There were over a hundred dwellings or lodges, called *hodenosotes,* made of elm bark. A lodge was from forty to sixty feet long. Inside, sleeping benches ran along the entire length of the side walls, with a row of fires down the center of the floor. Generally several families occupied each lodge.

In the gardens and fields of Saukenuk the women raised beans, pumpkins, squash, and so much corn that they had enough left over to use in trade. There were about eight hundred acres under cultivation. The gardens, and sometimes the lodges, were surrounded by fences supporting melon vines. The uncultivated land outside the village was covered with bluegrass, furnishing excellent pasturage for the horses. Wild berries, fruit, and nuts were gathered from the countryside. The men hunted for deer, buffalo, elk, bear, and wild fowl, and abundant supplies of fish were caught in the rapids where the Rock and Mississippi rivers met.

Though the village was a permanent settlement and the center of tribal life, it was not used all the year round. In September the inhabitants left for their hunting grounds, the women and children traveling in canoes, the men on horseback. Winter camps were set up, with lodges made of skins and of mats woven from reeds. Hunting went on until the weather grew too cold. Then the tribe passed the time pleasantly with games until it became mild enough to resume. As soon as the snow began to melt, the men went off on fur-trapping expeditions, for beaver, deer, muskrat, raccoon, mink, and otter. They exchanged the skins for guns and ammunition, knives, traps, pots and pans, blankets, cloth, wampum, paint—practically everything they needed aside from food and shelter. Like most eastern Indians, the Sac and Fox had become completely dependent upon the white man's goods. They even preferred tobacco cured by the white man's methods to the native product.

The fur trade was a vital part of their economy, as it was for most Indians in the Great Lakes region. Many thousands of dollars worth of furs were trapped every year by the Sac and Fox, who were considered the best hunters on the Mississippi and Missouri rivers. The white traders joined the Indians at their winter camps, and groups of Indians paid regular visits to the great fur center of St. Louis and to trading posts on the Great Lakes. The section of the Mississippi along which the Sac and Fox lived was part of the main water route of this immensely profitable trade. The tribes dealt with the Spanish, French, British, and after the Revolution, with the Americans, acquiring an intimate knowledge of these different nationalities in the process.

While the young men were off hunting, the others went on to the maple sugar camp, one of the most enjoyable events of the season. Wild fowl was plentiful, and the sugar making was accompanied by feasting. Then the entire village met at a prearranged point, and they all returned to Saukenuk. Here the caches of dried meat, fish, and vegetables, carefully wrapped and buried the previous fall, were dug up to provide food during the spring. Fences and lodges were mended, and planting begun.

After the corn was planted, the Crane Dance was held. It lasted two or three days, during which the young men courted the girls they wanted to marry. At the end of the first year of marriage the couple could separate if they were not happy together, and try again with someone else. "If we were to live together and disagree," said Black Hawk, "we should be as foolish as the whites."

The Crane Dance was followed by the National Dance, held in the large square of the village. After this the town broke up into groups again. The young men left to hunt buffalo and deer; some of the older men and women went away to work the lead mines. The mines owned by the two tribes were among the richest in the area. Several thousand pounds of ore were smelted each year and sold to white traders. Other groups went out to catch and dry fish or to gather reeds for making mats. When all the separate parties returned to town, they exchanged gifts of what they had caught, mined, gathered, or dried, so that everyone had an assortment of the town's goods.

Then the feasts and ceremonies, the visits, dances, and games really began. Almost every day one lodge or another gave a feast to celebrate some special event or in honor of the Great Spirit. Dramatic performances and new songs were prepared as part of the entertainment. When the corn was ripe, another feast was held, together with a great ceremony to give thanks for the harvest. There were also ball games—usually some form of lacrosse—with up to five hundred players on a side. Contests took place between villages and even between tribes, as well as between local teams, with everyone, players and spectators, gambling heavily on the results. The last item of the sports season was horse racing, again accompanied by gambling and feasting.

When all the corn had been harvested, preparations for the next season began. Food was dried and stored; canoes were loaded with supplies; and the town was ready to leave once more for winter quarters, to start the whole cycle over again. "In this way," said Black Hawk, "the year rolled around happily." It was a good life, providing intense satisfaction and fulfillment to the Indians. They saw no reason why it should not go on indefinitely. "The white people had plenty of land, and would never take our village from us."

But the white people did take it, and the effect was shattering. The agreeable, ordered round of work and pleasure would never return in quite the same way.

chapter two

Keokuk and Black Hawk

There were two outstanding men in Saukenuk: Keokuk and Black Hawk. Keokuk, whose name meant Watchful Fox, was a handsome, graceful man, a fine dancer and athlete, thirteen years younger than Black Hawk. He was the son of a half-French mother. He had not been born a chief, but his powers of oratory and leadership were recognized early, and he eventually became head chief of the tribe. He was a clever politician, skilled at dealing with the white authorities, who regarded him as one of the greatest Indian diplomats, a "very extraordinary man of a high order of talent." He was all for peace, doing whatever he could to keep his people from becoming involved in wars, especially hopeless ones with the white man.

Keokuk had a highly realistic view of the whites: though he resisted them at first, in time he recognized their superior strength, knew they had come to stay and would spread over the country, and realized that armed opposition was worse than useless. To resist, he felt, was only to lose more in the end. The wisest course was to meet peaceably with white leaders and try to get the best possible terms for the future existence of the tribe, even if the terms were not in themselves all that he would like.

Black Hawk was almost the exact opposite of Keokuk. His Indian name was Ma-ka-tai-me-she-kia-kiak, which meant Black Sparrow Hawk. Born in 1767, the same year as Andrew Jackson, he had a more rigidly traditional outlook than Keokuk. His appearance was impressive. He was lithe, broad-shouldered, with a well-shaped head and prominent cheekbones. The stern effect of his aquiline nose and dark piercing eyes was softened by what one observer called a "mild and benevolent expression." He was a famous warrior, noted for his fighting spirit, his courage, and his exploits in war. He was an astute military strategist, but lacked the calm judgment with which Keokuk handled the tribe's affairs. Keokuk was mild, polite, and self-possessed; Black Hawk was proud and headstrong. Keokuk was willing to compromise if he thought it would be best for the tribe in the long run; Black Hawk would rather take a desperate gamble for the sake of honor and patriotism.

In his own way, Keokuk was as patriotic, as bold, and as brave as Black Hawk, and capable of firm and decisive leadership. A white agent, seeing him at a council, said: "He stood as a prince, majestic and frowning," and with his high crest of feathers and daring eye looked "like another Coriolanus." He did not hesitate to fight when he thought it necessary or feasible. But he was cautious where Black Hawk was hasty to take action.

Keokuk was a shrewd judge of character, while Black Hawk was somewhat gullible, inclined to trust the wrong people. Keokuk could be filled with lively enthusiasm and welcomed new ideas; Black Hawk was more intense, deeply religious, and easily stirred by appeals to pride or tradition. They were both completely honest and extremely able men, but they represented two different viewpoints among the Indians: to accept as inevitable the advance of white civilization and adjust to the increasing restrictions and changing customs peacefully, or to resist and try to retain as much of the old land and old ways as possible.

Black Hawk neither liked nor trusted the Americans. He supported Tecumseh in his efforts to unite the tribes against the frontier settlers and led a group of Sac and Fox warriors to fight on the side of the English in the War of 1812. He was with Tecumseh when he fell at the Battle of the Thames. Keokuk remained neutral and urged the tribe to keep on peaceful terms with the Americans. Because of this he became known as the leader of the "Peace Band." Black Hawk, who cherished the tomahawk he inherited from Tecumseh, continued to prefer the English even after the War of 1812. His followers were called the "British Band."

These differences naturally led to great rivalry between the two leaders and the points of view they represented. The time would come when the tribe would have to choose between them.

chapter three

1804: The First Treaty

Black Hawk's distrust of Americans began in 1804, the year whose events laid the groundwork for the Black Hawk War. Until that year, Black Hawk had little direct contact with Americans. The whites with whom his tribe had close relations were the English in Canada and the Spanish in St. Louis. But the Louisiana Purchase in 1803 brought the hunting grounds of the Sac and Fox inside the boundaries of the United States.

Shortly before the Purchase, a treaty between Napoleon and the Spanish king had assigned the territory to France, but the French had still not taken control when it was sold to the United States. The official transfer ceremonies took place in March 1804 at St. Louis, the provincial capital of what was then called Upper Louisiana. On the first day of the ceremonies the territory was formally handed over by Spain to France, and on the second day it was transferred from France to the United States.

A large audience watched as the flags were changed, while the drums beat and the cannon fired off their salutes. One of the most absorbed spectators was Captain Meriwether Lewis, who had been appointed by President Thomas Jefferson to lead an expedition to the unexplored West and report back on the land and its native inhabitants. The members of the expedition, with Captain William Clark as second in command, had been assembling near St. Louis and were now almost ready to set off up the Missouri River.

Among the spectators, too, were a large number of Indians, including Black Hawk. The Sac were deeply concerned over the proceedings. Unlike other tribes in the area, the Sac had never signed a treaty with the United States. No definite boundaries had been set between the tribe's land and that of the Americans. Their relationship to the new government was uncertain; indeed their whole future had suddenly become uncertain.

The change was wholly unexpected. Black Hawk had come to St. Louis on a routine trading visit and was astonished to learn that in a few days the Americans would arrive to take over. The Sac had gotten along well with the Spanish and were dismayed at their departure. ". . . We should then lose our Spanish father!" wrote Black Hawk. "This news made myself and band sad—because we had always heard bad accounts of the Americans from Indians who had lived near them!—and we were sorry to lose our Spanish father, who had always treated us with great friendship."

After the American government became the new "father"

of the Indians, the British did everything they could to create misunderstanding and hostility between them. In this policy, the British started out with an advantage. After replacing the French, they had treated tribes like the Sac and Fox with great friendship, and a warm, close relationship had been firmly established long before the Americans took control. The British used to invite the Indians up to Canada, entertain them pleasantly at army and trading posts on the Great Lakes, and send them home with generous gifts. At the beginning of the hunting season, British traders extended full credit to the tribes, supplying all the necessary provisions and trapping equipment. Later, the traders came up to the hunting camps and the Indians gave them furs to pay for these advance supplies. The British, who greatly respected the trapping abilities of the Sac and Fox, found the trade highly lucrative. In their report, Lewis and Clark said the combined tribes caught ten thousand dollars worth of furs annually; this increased considerably in the years that followed.

A further bond between the British and the Sac and Fox was the support provided by the Indians during the Revolutionary War. They had helped the English against the Americans, and even after the war, had expressed their friendship and loyalty to the British in Canada. The Sac and Fox continued to pay frequent visits to the British posts to the great unease of the American government.

At the time of the Louisiana Purchase the British had a special reason for keeping the Indians stirred up against the Americans. The British were afraid that while their own armies were occupied against Napoleon in Europe, the Americans might try to seize part of Canada. The British Canadians hoped to use the Indians in two ways: to keep the Americans so busy dealing with native unrest that they would not have time to march against Canada, and to en-

courage the Indians to fight on the side of Canada in case
war did break out.

The Indians were still being used as pawns in the struggles
between white nations as they had been ever since the great
European powers began to divide up the American continent. And it was still turning out disastrously for the natives.

The United States also tried to use the Indians for its own
purposes. Warriors were offered money to fight for the
Americans. But since many Indians were reluctant to serve
against the British, the Americans provoked them into fighting each other. Tribes friendly to the United States were sent
to attack hostile or pro-British tribes.

One of the tribes used against the pro-British Indians was
the Osage. They got along unusually well with the Americans, incurring the jealousy of other tribes, who resented the
protection given the Osage by the United States Army. The
Sac, especially, were jealous of the Osage, who were traditional enemies. After the Americans occupied St. Louis,
word came to Saukenuk that these old enemies had been entertained there and presented with many gifts. Some hotheaded young Sacs became angry at both the Osage and the
Americans, who were showing such favoritism, and a small
band of these warriors went on a rampage.

They ran into a group of Americans, quarreled with them,
and three Americans were killed. The white settlers in the
area became alarmed and demanded protection against the
Indians. There was talk of taking revenge by destroying the
Sac villages near St. Louis. The Sac in their turn grew even
more alarmed. With the exception of a few young men, most
of the tribe wanted to establish peaceful relations with the
Americans. In order to prevent serious trouble from developing, they agreed to turn over to the white authorities one
of the young men who had taken part in the killing. A small

party of Sac and Fox were sent to St. Louis to surrender the guilty warrior.

Just before all this took place, William Henry Harrison, as governor of Indiana Territory and superintendent of Northwest Indian affairs, had been authorized to make a treaty with the Sac and Fox tribes. He hoped to persuade them to sign over a large portion of their land to the United States. Harrison was highly adept at coaxing land cessions from the Indians. During his regime, using threats, whisky, or the desperation of weak and hungry chiefs, he got the natives to part with some forty-eight million acres of land for a price of about one cent an acre.

He was in St. Louis when the Sac and Fox peace delegation arrived and decided this would be an opportune moment to press for a treaty and a land cession. He welcomed the Indians, gave them elaborate gifts and generous amounts of whisky, and asked them to sign a treaty. In their anxious —and probably drunken—state, they were glad to sign.

At this point a typical Indian confusion set in from which all the later trouble would arise. It was customary among Indians to recompense the relatives of victims killed by members of the tribe. The delegation sent to St. Louis had been authorized to make such a payment, in addition to handing over the accused warrior; it had *not* been authorized to give away tribal land. This was a matter requiring serious consideration and action by the entire tribal council. Generally a tribe expected to receive a formal invitation to discuss land transfers. Then, after careful advance discussion, a large delegation of the most important chiefs and orators, accompanied by many ordinary members of the tribe, would be sent. Long parleys were expected to take place, and by the time the treaty was signed, the whole tribe would have had a chance to learn its terms.

When the Americans had demanded that a delegation be

sent to discuss the killings, nothing was said about the sale of land. The tribe therefore sent only a small group consisting of five minor chiefs. Ordinarily this would have been enough for the purpose, but Harrison had taken advantage of the situation and cajoled these few, unrepresentative chiefs to sign away a vast area belonging to the tribe. All their land east of the Mississippi River and some of their hunting grounds on the west bank, fifteen million acres in all, were ceded to the United States in return for $2,234.50 already spent on the delegation and an annual payment in goods valued at $600 for the Sac and $400 for the Fox. The tract included large sections of the present state of Illinois and southern Wisconsin and a small piece of Missouri, and at that price, it was one of the biggest land bargains the United States ever got from the Indians.

Later, the warrior who was turned in was found to have killed in self-defense and was pardoned by President Jefferson. Before the pardon reached St. Louis, the young Indian tried to break out of jail—such close confinement was unbearable to Indians—and was fatally shot in the attempt.

When the delegation returned home and reported the events of their St. Louis trip, the rest of the tribe was shocked and confused. The delegates, having been drunk through most of their excursion, could barely remember what had happened, and many members of the tribe never fully understood or accepted the fact that their land had been sold. After all, the delegation had not been authorized to make such a sale.

At most, they might have thought that what had been ceded to the United States was not the land itself, containing their homes, but the right to use some of their hunting grounds. Like many Indians, they did not clearly understand the white man's legal concepts of land ownership. "Land," Black Hawk was to say later, "cannot be sold." Whoever lived upon a particular piece of earth and cultivated it had a right to it, until he voluntarily moved away. He might permit someone else to use it temporarily. But would the Indians, Black Hawk asked, have given away such a vast tract permanently for only a thousand dollars a year? He undoubtedly regarded this annuity as being the same as the annual gifts presented by the British, which had been given to the tribes as tokens of friendship, without any yielding of land in return.

But if the United States really intended to take the land away from the tribes, then, in the Indians' view, it had accomplished this purpose through an act of bad faith. A small delegation, sent for a specific and limited purpose, had been deliberately tricked into making a major land cession about which the entire tribe should have been consulted. The treaty of 1804, their first with the Americans, left the Sac and Fox disturbed and resentful, with a vague, foreboding sense of having been cheated.

chapter four

The War of 1812

In the years immediately following the treaty of 1804, the land was not yet needed by white settlers. According to the usual terms of such treaties, therefore, the Indians were permitted to remain for the time being. But the misunderstandings and distrust continued. Many Indians regarded the land as still belonging to them. There were sporadic flare-ups between the two races: occasional white settlers and hunters were attacked by Sac warriors; occasional Indians were assaulted by white frontiersmen. Detachments of the United States Army came through the area, arousing the suspicions of the Indians and adding to the atmosphere of hostility.

The official United States agent to the Sac, William Ewing, appointed early in 1805, confirmed Black Hawk's anxieties about the trustworthiness of the Americans. Ewing cheated both the government and the tribe in ways that were to become common among government agents: he persuaded the Indians to trade their guns to him in exchange for whisky, then sold the guns, which were vitally necessary for hunting food, back to the Indians at a much higher price. He sold the government corn provided for Indian use to private traders and put the money received into his own pocket. He bought supplies for his personal use and charged the cost to the government.

The Indians were puzzled by this kind of chicanery and defenseless against it. They had their own sharp bargaining practices, their own methods of outwitting a competitor or adversary; but outright dishonesty on the part of an official representative of a tribe or government was something else. It was a matter of great pride for a tribal leader to keep his word, and it was difficult for the Indians to understand that an agent of a powerful white government might betray the promises made by his superiors or stoop to petty cheating. By the time they realized they were being swindled, it was too late to prevent the fraud.

Though complaints were made against him by both Indians and white observers, the agent remained in office for more than two years. In 1807 General William Clark was appointed agent for all the tribes of the region. He was highly capable and honest, but a poor foundation for Indian-white relations had already been laid.

Between 1800 and 1809, more than a hundred million acres were taken from the Indians by means of threats or force or, as with the Sac and Fox, by dealing with a few unauthorized members of a tribe. Though there were still not enough white settlers to require the immediate use of all this territory, they were nevertheless entering it at an astonishing rate. The Indians watched in consternation as the country about them began filling up with American farms and villages. A white settlement, said the Indians, is like a spot of raccoon grease on a new blanket. You do not realize how wide and fast the tiny stain will spread.

Like the other tribes in the area, the Sac and Fox were upset by this invasion of their homeland. It is possible that the Indians of the Great Lakes and upper Mississippi might have withdrawn more or less peacefully before the pressure of advancing white settlement, as many of the eastern tribes had done. But there was no place for these Indians to retreat. Just behind them were the powerful Sioux and Chippewa, blocking off any movement to the west in search of new homes and hunting grounds.

Caught between the rapidly approaching whites from the east and the hostile tribes cutting them off to the west, there seemed no alternative but to remain where they were and defend their homes. When Tecumseh began to organize an Indian confederacy to stem the white influx, the Sac and Fox, and especially Black Hawk, were ready to listen to the arguments of the eloquent Shawnee. Though the Sac and Fox did not become an important part of Tecumseh's organization, they remained stirred up by his activities and showed increasing hostility toward the United States. The Americans responded to this hostility by building Fort Madison in Sac territory. The presence of the garrison only added to the tension between the tribes and the American government.

When the War of 1812 broke out, Tecumseh joined the British in Canada, but the Sac and Fox hesitated. Both the British and Americans tried to win the aid or at least neutrality of the tribes. Most of the Indians, fearful of the powerful —and threatening—Americans, were cautiously inclined to stay out of the war. Even Black Hawk, who actively preferred the British, remained neutral until an American blunder goaded him into resentful action.

In the contest between the two white powers for Indian friendship, British traders played an important and carefully planned role. They gave the Indians far better trading terms than the Americans did. Numerous gifts were presented whenever natives went up to visit Canadian trading posts. An Indian could expect to receive arms and ammunition, blankets, tobacco, pipes, and articles of clothing. The Americans, on the contrary, gave very few gifts. Worst of all, they extended no credit to the Indians in advance of the hunting season.

The British provided tribesmen with ammunition, traps, and food supplies at the beginning of the fur hunting expeditions. After the furs were trapped, the Indians would give the traders enough of the skins to pay for the supplies, and then exchange the rest for additional goods. The American traders refused to provide supplies without immediate payment. This made it impossible for the Indians, who had no cash reserves, to carry on their hunting. Their medium of exchange was not money but furs, and first the furs had to be caught. How did the Americans expect them to go out and get the furs, they asked, without equipment?

This whole matter of credit was the basis for a serious misunderstanding between the United States and the Indians. The young American government did not understand just how essential the credit system had become to the welfare of the natives. Without it, they would suffer. The British, on the other hand, understood this very well, indeed had sponsored the system for many years. Upon it rested the whole economic structure of the fur-trading tribes.

Just before the outbreak of war, a group of Midwestern chiefs, including some from the Sac and Fox, were invited to Washington to meet President James Madison, as part of the American attempt to win over the Indians. Madison persuaded them to stop trading with the British and sell their furs to American traders instead. During the discussion the

Indians had understood, perhaps incorrectly because of poor translation, that the American traders would follow the British custom of giving them hunting supplies in advance, on credit.

The chiefs returned home with this information, and the Sac and Fox hunters went to see the American trader. No one, however, had told the trader what Madison was supposed to have said, and to the dismay of the Indians, he refused to give them anything on credit. "All was gloom and discontent!" said Black Hawk. The tribe did not know how they would get through the hunting season, and few of them slept that night. But the next day the British sent two boatloads of supplies—on credit—together with gifts of pipes and tobacco, wampum, a large silk flag, and a keg of rum.

The principal British trader for the Sac and Fox was Robert Dickson, who was regarded with great respect and affection by his native customers. Along with the supplies sent at this time was a warm personal message from Dickson.

Black Hawk needed no further proof that his best interests lay not with the Americans but with the British. When it was suggested by the Canadian agent who brought the supplies that Black Hawk might want to help the war effort of his good friends, the grateful chief quickly agreed. He claimed later that the failure of the American trader to carry out Madison's promise had ended all hope of remaining at peace, that he was *"forced into* WAR *by being* DECEIVED!"

Most of the Sac and Fox still refused to fight against the Americans, but Black Hawk was able to gather a war party of more than two hundred and lead them to Green Bay, where he was appointed chief of five hundred Indians from the whole region. From there he and his braves went on to Detroit to join Tecumseh and the British troops to which he was attached.

With Black Hawk and so many warriors absent, the remaining tribesmen grew concerned about what would happen in case of an American attack. It was decided that some of the chiefs should take a group of old men, women, and children—about fifteen hundred people altogether—to St. Louis and put themselves under the protection of the Americans. General William Clark, now governor of Missouri Territory, was happy to receive them. Such tribal divisions made it easier for government authorities to control the natives. He sent them west of the Mississippi, a little way up the Missouri River, where they set up new villages.

Some time afterward, a party of one hundred American soldiers led by Major Nathan Boone, Daniel Boone's son, began to march in the general direction of Saukenuk. Fearful of an attack, the village leaders called a council and decided that the remaining inhabitants should leave Saukenuk and join those who had left earlier.

Until then, Keokuk had been of little importance in the tribe. He had never killed an enemy and so, according to tribal custom, was not permitted to enter the council lodge. He stood outside the door and when he heard the decision, asked that he be allowed to enter and address the council. The elders were astonished but let him do so. The young man made an impassioned speech, sharply criticizing the chiefs for their willingness to fly at the approach of an enemy. "Give me charge of your warriors," he cried, "I will defend the village, and you may sleep in safety!"

The chiefs were so impressed that they appointed Keokuk a war chief on the spot. He planned a careful defense, sending out spies and advance patrols, one of which he led himself. As it happened, Boone's party turned back before reaching Saukenuk, but Keokuk's bravery, eloquence, and strategic skill were recognized by the tribe. When Black Hawk returned that fall, he found that Keokuk had become a serious rival.

The following year the war came a good deal closer to

Saukenuk. In June 1814 the Americans started to build a
fort at the trading town of Prairie du Chien, where the Wisconsin River joins the Mississippi. Several boatloads of
American soldiers under Major John Campbell were sent up
from St. Louis, to help man the fort when it was finished. But
on July 20, with Campbell still on the way, British forces attacked and seized the unfinished fort, which they renamed
Fort McKay. Early the next morning Campbell's boat was
blown by gale winds into the shallow waters off an island in
the Mississippi. He decided to land on the island and wait
until the wind died down. Almost immediately Campbell's
group was attacked by Sac warriors led by Black Hawk.
Troops in the other boats heard the gunfire and came to
Campbell's aid.

Black Hawk was acting under orders from the British,
who had supplied him with four kegs of gunpowder. In the
battle that took place among the hazel and willow bushes of
Campbell's Island, as it came to be called, fourteen Americans were killed and seventeen wounded. One keelboat was
burned, and the others were forced to turn back down the
Mississippi.

The Americans, greatly disturbed by the loss of their fort
at Prairie du Chien, were furious at this added defeat. In revenge for Black Hawk's attack on Campbell, a detachment
of 430 men led by Major Zachary Taylor was sent to destroy
the Sac villages. In August the twenty-nine-year-old Taylor
—who would be known much later as "Old Rough and
Ready"—set out with his men in eight boats. As news of his
approach spread, Indians of the neighboring tribes, including Winnebagos and even the generally hostile Sioux, went
to Saukenuk to offer their help to Black Hawk. About 1000
braves prepared to hold off the Americans. The British at
Prairie du Chien sent 30 men armed with three pieces of artillery—a three-pounder cannon and two swivels.

Zachary Taylor had planned to summon the Indians to a council, and then attack them as they met, unprepared for fighting, on the council grounds. But when he raised his flag of truce, the suspicious natives refused to respond. They gathered along the river bank, or paddled their canoes a safe distance away from Taylor's guns. Shortly before dawn the next morning the Indians attacked. Taylor seemed to be conducting a successful defense when suddenly the British, whose presence had been unsuspected till this moment, opened fire with their heavy guns. The surprise shelling was so effective that Taylor was forced to retreat. The Sac villages were saved, and once again the Americans had been defeated.

These victories over the United States Army made Black Hawk feel that with British help he could hold off any American invasion of Sac territory. But the following year his confidence in the British was seriously shaken. Early in 1815 he was shocked to learn that the British had admitted to losing the war and had signed a peace treaty. He refused to agree that the Americans had won and announced that he would "continue to fight them till they are off our lands." But after a few skirmishes fought without British support, he too was forced to admit defeat. He went back to Saukenuk, to find other disappointments waiting for him.

During the latter part of the war, Keokuk had worked out his attitude toward the Americans. He was prepared to fight them if necessary, but had decided that it was wiser to negotiate. Shrewder and more far-sighted than Black Hawk, Keokuk realized that the Americans were now the major power confronting the Indians. While Black Hawk was fighting on the side of the British, Keokuk managed to convince the United States that most of the tribe had peaceful intentions. By the time Black Hawk returned to Saukenuk,

Keokuk was established as leader of the pro-American peace group. He was acknowledged as an important chief by white authorities and treated by them with friendship and respect. The disgruntled Black Hawk had to be content with his role as leader of the smaller "British Band." He was certainly unloved by the Americans and received none of the gifts that they began to lavish upon Keokuk. The most unfortunate result of this rivalry and of the war itself was the split that developed within the tribe as its members lined up behind one or the other of the contending chiefs.

Equally unfortunate was the treaty forced upon the tribe in 1816, which reaffirmed the treaty of 1804. Black Hawk was induced to join the treaty conference by a promise of pardon for his hostile actions during the War of 1812. Together with the other chiefs, he put his cross to the document after being threatened with war, but later insisted that he had not understood the exact terms of the treaty. "Here, for the first time, I touched the goose quill to the treaty—not knowing, however, that by that act, I consented to give away my village. Had that been explained to me, I should have opposed it, and never would have signed their treaty. . . ."

Once again a treaty was signed without a clear understanding of just what was involved. Many Indians "touched the goose quill" without knowing exactly to what they were agreeing, especially since few could understand much English, let alone read it. "What do we know of the manner of the laws and customs of the white people?" asked Black Hawk. "They might buy our bodies for dissection, and we would touch the goose quill to confirm it, without knowing what we were doing. This was the case with myself and people in touching the goose quill the first time."

Despite the signing of the treaty and despite Keokuk's repeated assurances of friendship, the United States still distrusted the Sac and Fox. To prepare against possible trouble, the American Army built Fort Armstrong on Rock Island, about three miles north of Saukenuk. Black Hawk did not object to the fort itself, but he was sorry to see it placed on "the best island on the Mississippi," an island that the Sac villagers had been using as a garden, "which supplied us with strawberries, blackberries, gooseberries, plums, apples, and nuts of different kinds; and its waters supplied us with fine fish." He was disturbed by the white man's failure to respect the island's resident spirit, near whose particular cave the Indians had been careful not to make any noise. "In my early life, I spent many happy days on this island. A good spirit had care of it. . . . But the noise of the fort has since driven him away, and no doubt a *bad spirit* has taken his place!"

Black Hawk had returned from St. Louis, where the treaty conference was held in May, to find that work on the fort had already begun. To his sadness in seeing still another of his favorite spots taken over by the whites, there were soon added two deeply personal tragedies. First, his beloved eldest son became ill and died. Shortly afterward, his youngest daughter, "an interesting and affectionate child," also died. In his grief he gave away all his belongings and left the village. With his wife, Singing Bird, and remaining children, he withdrew to the isolation of a lodge built in the middle of his cornfield. There he lived for two years in a state of mourning, blacking his face and eating only one meal, consisting of a little boiled corn, a day. He hoped that after all the disasters he had endured, the Great Spirit would be moved by such self-denial and "would take pity on me."

chapter five

The Uneasy Years

The years following the war were filled with strain. As more settlers came west, more pressure was applied to the Indians to clear out and yield the land to the arriving whites. Some of the Sac and Fox gave way and sought new hunting grounds in the northwest, only to run head-on into the Sioux. The result was savage warfare between the tribes, with occasional harm to white settlers who got in the way. United States authorities tried to establish peace, with little success.

Hunting became more difficult, not only because of the Sioux but because, as settlers entered the area, the game moved away. The presence of so many people, the clearing away of the woodlands, drove off the wild animals. The Indians had to travel greater and greater distances—sometimes as much as three hundred miles—to find suitable game.

There were increasing disputes between tribal leaders and Federal agents over the exact boundaries of the land involved in the treaties. In 1824 a party of Sac and Fox chiefs, including Keokuk but not Black Hawk, were invited to Washington to discuss boundary problems and the conflict with the Sioux. Some agreement was reached on the boundaries, but nothing could be done about the Sioux.

After the conference the chiefs were taken on a tour to impress them with the strength of the United States and the futility of opposing it. They visited Baltimore, Philadelphia, and New York. Keokuk returned home more than ever convinced of the need for coming to terms with the unconquerable white man. He accepted the prospect of leaving Saukenuk and moving farther west, despite the presence of the Sioux. It was easier to fight them than the whites, and the American government might even help to prevent such conflict.

Black Hawk, however, refused to leave Saukenuk. Perhaps it was a mistake not to have included him in the eastern trip. If, like Keokuk, he had seen the real size of the United States, he might have been less defiant. But he had never been to any town larger than St. Louis and had little conception of just how formidable white power was.

The split between the rivals deepened. The whole tribe talked of nothing except whether to move west with Keokuk or to remain and defend their homes with Black Hawk. The American authorities, naturally preferring Keokuk's attitude, continued to give him lavish gifts and to acknowledge him as the principal leader of the combined tribes. If Keokuk had a visible fault as a dedicated leader, it was his love of possessions and his pleasure in making a fine appearance. A fancy coat, a silk handkerchief, an American saddle, and similar tokens from his American friends probably did nothing to weaken his conviction that it would be foolish to antagonize the whites. There was nevertheless little truth in Black Hawk's accusation that Keokuk enjoyed the attention of the American authorities so much that he was "willing to barter our rights merely for the good opinion of the whites."

Black Hawk continued to visit the British in Canada. He still regarded them as his friends and possible allies. But the British presents were now meager, and the British insistence on remaining at peace with the United States was discouraging. Nevertheless, though Keokuk cut an increasingly dashing and impressive figure, many tribesmen were moved by Black Hawk's stubborn courage in announcing his intention of remaining in Saukenuk at all costs.

In the meantime the white settlements came steadily closer, and clashes between natives and whites grew more frequent. Indian women entering tribal fields found them occupied by settlers who beat them and drove them off; braves riding along old tribal paths that now ran between white farms were attacked. In spite of the government ban, whites sold liquor to Indians, got them drunk, and then collected many times the value of the drink in horses and furs. An Indian who took honey from a hive was told that the bee tree now belonged to a white man. He offered to return the honey, but the whites took his entire winter's catch of furs instead. Black Hawk himself was accused of killing some hogs. Though he denied it, the whites refused to listen and beat him severely with sticks. "How could we like such people who treated us so unjustly?" he asked.

The Indians angrily resented such treatment and wanted to attack the settlers in return. Keokuk urged them to be patient and to prepare for moving west, but many of the younger braves preferred Black Hawk's position of defiance.

Toward the end of the 1820s, interracial friction became so great that the governor of Illinois decided the time had come for the Indians to get off the lands which by earlier treaties had been ceded to the United States. In the spring of 1828, Governor Ninian Edwards wrote a sharp letter to Washington, saying that if the Federal government did not remove the Indians immediately, the local authorities would do it themselves.

Local action would undoubtedly be harsher than any methods used by Federal agents. Ninian Edwards' sentiments toward the Indians had been demonstrated during the War of 1812 when, as territorial governor, he signed an act "to promote retaliation upon hostile Indians." Parties of whites traveling in hostile territory would receive a reward of one hundred dollars for killing an Indian warrior or taking a squaw or child prisoner. Rangers would be paid fifty dollars for the same acts, if performed by a party of no more than fifteen.

The Superintendent of Indian Affairs, General William Clark, thought it would be better all around to handle the matter of Indian removal himself rather than leave it to Governor Edwards. Clark agreed to have all the Indians, except for a few Kickapoos, out of Illinois by May 25, 1829.

He began pressing the tribes to move as soon as possible. The Sac and Fox objected; they had already planted their corn and did not want to lose the harvest. Some, including Black Hawk, insisted that the area which contained the village of Saukenuk was not part of the ceded lands. But they were mistaken: Saukenuk had been included in the Treaty of 1804. Now all the misunderstandings and confusions connected with that document would be revealed.

Unhappy parleys took place, yet nothing was definitely

settled. Keokuk had been persuaded to abandon Saukenuk, but no exact date was set. When the tribe went off to their winter hunting camp in the season of 1828–29, some whites mistakenly thought they were leaving for good and moved into the town. Black Hawk, hearing of this invasion, returned to the village from the camp, a distance that took him ten days to walk. Back in Saukenuk he found a white family living in his own lodge. Through an interpreter he explained that the village still belonged to the tribe, which would be returning in the spring, and asked the whites to be gone by then. He walked back to the winter camp feeling confident that the trespassers would quit Saukenuk.

But when the tribe returned in spring, they were appalled to find that the whites had not left, that indeed more had moved in. Some of the lodges had been destroyed or badly damaged. Fences had been built around the best cornfields. Black Hawk's lodge was still occupied by whites, who refused to leave.

The distressed Indians hurried to their agent to protest the seizure of their village. The agent at this time was Thomas Forsyth, a former trader and frontiersman who had been appointed by the Indian Bureau in 1816. He was a good agent and well disposed toward the Indians, but when the Sac insisted that the whites must be forced to leave Saukenuk, he reminded the tribe of the Treaty of 1804. Black Hawk replied that this treaty, unfairly obtained to begin with, did not include Saukenuk, nor did any of the later treaties. This was the same argument that had been gone over in all the earlier councils but had never been cleared up to the satisfaction of the Indians. Once again they were assured that the treaties included Saukenuk. Black Hawk retorted that the whites always said one thing to the Indians but put another on paper. The most he would concede was that some foolish and unauthorized chiefs might have signed a paper, but he and his band had not been consulted and were therefore not bound by it.

The white settlers also put pressure on Forsyth, demanding that he order the Indians to leave at once. There were incidents and complaints from both sides almost every day. A white man plowed up an Indian's cornfield, and when the Indian protested, the white hit him with a bean pole. When the Indians planted new cornfields, the whites turned their cattle into the fields to trample and ruin the corn. The Indians, in retaliation, let down the fence rails around the white men's corn and drove the cattle into their fields. Quarrels, threats, beatings, were constantly occurring. And all the time the illegal whisky trade continued, with the whites making the Indians drunk and then cheating them out of horses, guns, and hunting equipment. Black Hawk tried to talk to the whites, begging them not to sell whisky to the young braves, but the whites refused to stop.

Forsyth lacked the authority to do anything about the situation. Andrew Jackson had already declared that no state should have to put up with Indians inside its borders. The policy of removing the eastern tribes to new areas west of the Mississippi had been accepted in Washington, though the Removal Act itself had not yet been passed. All Forsyth could do was to tell the Indians that sooner or later they would have to leave Saukenuk.

Most of the tribe, under the leadership of Keokuk, though deeply unhappy about leaving, nevertheless resigned themselves to the move. But they did not want to go until they had gathered a last corn crop to tide them over in their new home. Forsyth had no way of forcing them to leave earlier, nor did he want to. His sympathies were with the Indians. "It appears hard to me," he wrote to General Clark, "that the Indian property should be stolen, their huts torn and burned down, and their persons insulted. . . ." He saw no reason why the whites should not wait until the Indians could gather their crops. It was only a matter of a few months. Furthermore, the whites were really illegal squatters—"intruders," said Forsyth—since the land had not yet been formally put up for sale.

But the settlers were impatient and appealed to authorities higher than Forsyth. These authorities, particularly the governor of Illinois and the Secretary of War, decided in favor of the whites and demanded that the Sac leave immediately. They also ordered that Saukenuk and the land around it be put up for sale to white settlers without further delay.

In making these decisions, Governor Edwards and Secretary Eaton had forgotten or ignored the fact that in order to move west, the Sac would have to invade the territory of the unfriendly Sioux. They were soon reminded of the difficulty, however, when a new series of hostile incidents broke out between the Sioux and the Sac and Fox. Other tribes, especially the Menominee and Winnebago, became involved, and it soon looked as though a general Indian war might break out.

More parleys and councils were held. After much discussion and irritation on all sides, new agreements were reached, new treaties signed. In the summer of 1830 the Sac and Fox, Sioux, Menominee, Iowa, Oto, Omaha, and Winnebago were prodded by the United States agents into a declaration of intertribal peace. They were also coaxed into giving the United States a huge tract of land between the Mississippi and Missouri Rivers. This was parceled out among the tribes for hunting grounds, so that now, presumably, the Sac could move west of the Mississippi without further trouble from the Sioux.

Keokuk did not return to Saukenuk in 1830. He established a new village on the Iowa River, but Black Hawk still

refused to leave his town. Keokuk tried to convince the "mu-
tinous Indians" to join the rest in their new home, but Black
Hawk scornfully refused. He considered Keokuk "a coward
and no brave, to abandon his village to be occupied by
strangers. What *right* had these people to our village, and
our fields, which the Great Spirit had given us to live upon?
. . . *Land cannot be sold*. The Great Spirit gave it to his
children to live upon, and cultivate . . . and so long as
they occupy and cultivate it, they have the right to the
soil. . . ."

The last sentence reads like the white man's argument that
God intended the land to belong to those who cultivated the
soil and made it fruitful. This was the excuse, from the time
of the Pilgrims, for taking land away from the natives. But
when the Indians themselves used the same reasoning, the
whites rejected it. If Black Hawk was convinced that he had
an inalienable right to the land, the white settlers felt they
had an equal, if not a higher, right. They moved in without
regard for the beliefs or feelings of the Indian occupants and
took over the Indians' cultivated fields for themselves.

Most of the tribe went with Keokuk; about one sixth remained with Black Hawk. Now the tribe was really torn
apart. The majority felt, with Keokuk, that resistance to the
whites was useless and would only lead to greater misfor-
tune. Black Hawk, though already in his sixties, was determined to resist. He firmly believed that he was right and insisted that his views be respected. Stubborn, unyielding, and
supremely confident of his military skill, he was willing to
take on the whole United States, if necessary, in a final effort
to obtain justice.

chapter six

Preliminaries to War

When Black Hawk decided to go back to Saukenuk after the winter hunt of 1830–31, despite all the urgings and warnings against his return, he knew there would be more trouble with the whites. He felt it might be wise to look for advice and help in advance. The most obvious source for this was the Federal agent at Rock Island, but the sympathetic and capable Forsyth had just been replaced by Felix St. Vrain, a man with no experience in the field at all. St. Vrain was completely baffled by the impasse between white and Indian demands, did not know what to do or say, and so did and said nothing.

Black Hawk turned to his British friends in Canada. He went to the British post at Malden, where he was told that if

Saukenuk had not been specifically included in the original treaty, the American authorities would not throw the natives out of their homes. Since Black Hawk was certain that the town had not been named, he returned from Malden in the fall of 1830 feeling greatly encouraged.

His principal source of advice was an Indian named Wabokieshiek, or White Cloud, half Winnebago, half Sac, who was considered a prophet. He lived in a Winnebago village on the Rock River. The Prophet was an imposing man, more than six feet tall, with deep-set eyes and a black moustache—a rare sight among Indians, who generally removed all facial hair. He was shrewd and intense, and filled with misleading advice that the credulous Black Hawk followed with unfortunate results. The Prophet kept assuring Black Hawk that the Winnebago, together with the Chippewa, Potawatomi, and Ottawa, would help the Sac in any struggle to keep their village. He added the undoubtedly false information that the British had agreed to send arms and provisions if a military defense of the town became necessary and had offered a refuge in Canada if the Indians were defeated.

Assisting in passing on such misinformation was Neapope, Black Hawk's chief aide in the British Band. He was one of the leading Sac chiefs, about thirty years old at the time, vigorous, clever, bold, a courageous and powerful warrior but scheming and unreliable. He and the Winnebago Prophet were as responsible as any other factor in bringing on the war, by pumping Black Hawk full of unwarranted encouragement and conveying nonexistent promises of help.

In 1830 there appeared another man who was to help set off the war. This was the newly elected governor of Illinois, John Reynolds, the "Old Ranger." Governor Reynolds had been raised on the frontier, had fought in a ranger company in the War of 1812, and had the usual frontiersman's dislike of Indians. He believed they were hopelessly savage, could never adapt to civilization, and the sooner they were replaced by white settlers the better. Whenever the settlers complained about the Sacs who were trying to return to Saukenuk, his first impulse was to call out the militia and drive the Indians away.

But General Edmund Gaines, commander of the Western Department of the regular United States Army, was against using the reckless and undisciplined militia. When Black Hawk returned to Saukenuk in the spring of 1831 and Reynolds threatened to take action, Gaines quickly intervened. He called a council at Rock Island with both Black Hawk and Keokuk and their divided followers.

Black Hawk's band attended in war paint, heavily armed, and openly hostile. Gaines informed the band that they must now leave Saukenuk for good, under the terms of the treaty of 1804. Black Hawk replied angrily that the treaty had been unauthorized and that when, in 1818, he had discovered that the annual "gifts" from the United States were not really outright gifts but payments for the land supposedly sold in 1804, he and his band had refused to accept the goods. They were therefore, insisted Black Hawk, not bound by the falsely secured treaty.

Keokuk did not agree with this. He asked Gaines to give him time to persuade Black Hawk's band to join him in his new village west of the Mississippi. That night he went among them and succeeded in convincing almost fifty families to leave the militant group and settle in the new village.

Meanwhile, Black Hawk consulted the Winnebago Prophet and was given the usual misleading advice. Resist, urged the Prophet, remain in your old village, and if it comes to outright war, the Winnebago and other tribes will quickly come to your assistance. Furthermore, he added, the whites would not really remove you by force. They are only trying to frighten you into thinking they will, so that you will leave of your own accord.

After convincing Black Hawk that other tribes would definitely help him in any military resistance, the Prophet then urged the Winnebago to agree to fight with the Sac band. But they were unresponsive, in spite of the Prophet's assurances to Black Hawk.

When Gaines heard about the Prophet's actions and advice, he felt it was useless to rely any further upon Keokuk. The persuasive reasoning of the peaceful chief might win over a part of Black Hawk's band, but the hard core of hostiles would remain and might even start a new frontier war. Gaines now believed that it might be best to remove the remaining Indians from Saukenuk by force if necessary, and decided to use Governor Reynolds' militia after all. He asked the Governor for fourteen hundred men, hoping that under the watchful leadership of the regular army, the militiamen might be properly controlled and be of some value in convincing the natives that the United States was serious about their removal.

The volunteer militiamen proved as undisciplined as Gaines had feared, and with so much hatred of Indians that "it required much gentle persuasion to restrain them from killing, indiscriminately, all the Indians they met." Keokuk's followers, who had voluntarily given up their homes to maintain good relations with the whites, were in as much danger from the militiamen as the resistant band of Black Hawk.

The plan was for the militia to attack Saukenuk from the south side of the Rock River while the regular troops came overland, pinning the Indians down between them. But when at dawn on June 26 the troops rushed into the town, they found it completely empty except for one old moth-eaten dog. Black Hawk and his band had slipped away during the night and crossed to the other side of the Mississippi. The militiamen were so furious at finding no Indians to attack that they set fire to the lodges, opened the Indian graves in the cemetery, scattered the bones, and wrecked everything else that came their way. Even the property of the whites who had moved into Saukenuk, and whom the militiamen were supposed to be protecting, was destroyed. The cure, to some settlers, seemed worse than the disease. The impatient, short-tempered volunteers had ripped up and burned the whites' fence rails, trampled the crops, and had done altogether, said one settler, ten times the damage caused by the Indians.

The next day General Gaines summoned the Indians to another council at Rock Island. At first Black Hawk refused to come. Gaines, thoroughly exasperated, said he would pursue Black Hawk and bring him in by force. Keokuk went to see him and added his pleas to Gaines's threats. At last Black Hawk reluctantly appeared. He even more reluctantly signed an agreement to leave Saukenuk forever.

It is difficult to know just what had changed the fiery chief's mind. Perhaps it was the unexpected show of strength put on by Gaines, or the violence of the rampaging militia, or perhaps even the sober, sensible arguments of Keokuk. Perhaps he finally realized that further resistance was useless. But that he had retreated from his rigid position was made clear by the subdued manner in which he entered the council house. For whatever reason he was now, he said, "determined to live in peace."

The terms of the "Articles of Agreement and Capitulation" were sad and humiliating for Black Hawk. He had to accept the authority of Keokuk, move west of the Mississippi and never cross back east without permission, and stop all communication with the British. In return for signing the agreement, Gaines promised to give Black Hawk's band the same amount of corn that they were being forced to abandon in the Saukenuk cornfields. Because of this, the agreement was known as "the Corn Treaty."

Unfortunately Gaines put the execution of his promise into the wrong hands, a common government error in dealing with Indians. He selected a group of the white Saukenuk settlers to decide how much corn should be provided. These men, grudging any food at all for Indians, sent far too little. Black Hawk's band, with no new crops available, went hungry. "Loud lamentations were heard," wrote Black Hawk, ". . . by our women and children, for their roasting-ears, beans, and squashes." One night a group of young men decided to cross the river and steal into Saukenuk secretly, to recover some of their own corn. But they were discovered and driven back with gunfire.

The same thing happened when a group of Sacs, this time with permission, returned to Saukenuk to rebury the bodies disturbed by the militiamen. The settlers prevented the Indians from getting near the graves, seized or destroyed their canoes, and fired upon the occupants.

Though Black Hawk and his followers had decided to live in peace, the inadequate corn ration and the interference with the reburial revived their suspicions about the white man's justice. Here were two promises broken as soon as they were made. How could such people be trusted? How could one live in peace with them?

These events had concerned the Sac branch of the combined tribes, but about a month after the Corn Treaty was signed, new trouble arose, involving the Fox. Some time earlier a party of Menominees and Sioux had attacked the Fox, killing several chiefs. Now, at the end of July 1831, the Fox saw a chance to retaliate. A band of young Foxes, assisted by some Sac braves—about a hundred men altogether— attacked a camp of Menominees and killed most of them.

Though this was a case of Indian killing Indian, the white settlers of Illinois were nevertheless frightened by the presence of armed braves on the warpath. They might be killing each other today was the general feeling, but tomorrow they might turn and kill *us!* The whites became even more stirred up when the Sioux, angered by the killing of two of their tribe by the Sac and Fox, announced their intention of fighting the combined tribes unless the white government took action. The clamor for protection against the Indians reached Washington where President Jackson demanded that the guilty Sac and Fox warriors be handed over immediately to the United States authorities.

On September 5, 1831, an Indian-white council was held at Fort Armstrong on Rock Island to discuss the matter. Black Hawk attended but said little. Keokuk did all the talking. The eloquent younger chief accused the American government of showing favoritism to some tribes—many similar intertribal killings had been ignored—and of maintaining a double standard for Indians and whites. Did not the white government execute murderers? And carry on wars? "Why do you not let us fight? You whites are constantly fighting. . . . why do you not let us be as the Great Spirit made us? and let us settle our own difficulties?"

Keokuk added that the tribe could not forcibly hand the killers over to the white authorities. According to Indian custom, the guilty men must give themselves up. And since many of the warriors involved had already left for distant hunting grounds, nothing could be done for the present.

Yet the American officers at the council left with the impression that, given time, Keokuk would persuade the guilty warriors to surrender. They decided to wait before taking further action. And, indeed, Keokuk might have talked the braves into giving themselves up. He had personally been opposed to their assault on the Menominees. But the young Foxes went instead to consult Black Hawk, who praised them for taking what he considered honorable vengeance against the murderers of their chiefs. President Jackson, he said, had taken no action against the Menominees the year before, for decoying and slaughtering the Fox chiefs. Why did he now demand the surrender of the Fox braves who had simply been punishing the murderers? "If he had no right in the first instance, he had none now," said Black Hawk; in any case, "where a difference exists between two nations," Jackson had no right to interfere.

The young Foxes, delighted with this view of their case, decided to remain as part of Black Hawk's band, greatly increasing its strength. Black Hawk, who had considered himself as having retired from active warfare and settled down to an old age of peace, began to feel a resurgence of his fighting spirit. The feeling grew even stronger when just at this time Neapope returned from a long summer visit to Canada with encouraging news.

According to Neapope, the British had again declared that unless the Sac had specifically sold their village, the Americans had no right to make the Indians leave. He added that the British promised to help the Sac resist any attempt at a forced removal.

Neapope also reported that on the way home he had visited the Winnebago Prophet, who affirmed that the British had promised guns, ammunition, and other necessary provisions in case of war. The Prophet said, too, that the Chippewa, Ottawa, and Potawatomi had agreed to help the Sac and Fox in any struggle against the whites. And finally, the Prophet said, still according to Neapope, the British had again offered a refuge in Canada if the Indians were defeated.

This news, together with Black Hawk's resentment at the failure of the whites to supply enough corn and the interference with the reburial, was enough to end his plans for peaceful retirement. The possibility of returning to his be-

loved Saukenuk could not be ignored. He began to talk of
going back there the following spring.

When Keokuk heard this, he was furious. He denounced
Neapope and the Prophet, insisting their information was
false. At best they had dangerously exaggerated or misunderstood the offers of help. No one, said Keokuk, would
come to the aid of any group rash enough to oppose the
overwhelming military strength of the United States. But, as
though to disprove Keokuk's words, Kickapoos, Winnebagos, and Potawatomis began to drift in to join Black
Hawk's band. That these few dissident members did not represent the majority of their tribes never occurred to Black
Hawk. Their presence was all he needed to rebuff Keokuk.

Badly upset at seeing his peacekeeping efforts destroyed
by a few irresponsible and hotheaded tribesmen, Keokuk
asked General Clark for permission to go to Washington.
Perhaps, he thought, if he could discuss the situation directly
with President Jackson or Secretary of War Cass, serious
trouble might be avoided. But Keokuk was denied the necessary permission, and Black Hawk went ahead with his plans.

Keokuk next asked George Davenport, the white trader to
whom the Sac and Fox sold their furs and a close friend of
Keokuk, to intercede for him. Davenport, on a trip to Washington, tried to approach President Jackson but failed. Jackson kept insisting that before any further discussion could be
held, the Sac and Fox must first surrender the braves who
had killed the Menominees. He was afraid that unless this
was done soon, the Menominee and Sioux would carry out
their threat to attack the combined tribes and a general Indian war would result.

An uneasy winter followed. Along the upper Mississippi,
the Sioux and Menominee and their allies prepared to attack the Sac and Fox. The Sac and Fox prepared to defend
themselves. And Black Hawk prepared to return to Saukenuk.

chapter seven

Return and Betrayal

All winter long Keokuk pleaded, argued, threatened against the return to Saukenuk, but Black Hawk refused to listen. He was too keyed up by the encouraging reports that continued to arrive from the Winnebago Prophet and Nea-pope, assuring him of British aid. He was so confident of re-gaining Saukenuk that he urged his tribesmen to abandon Keokuk and the unsatisfactory new settlement, and go back with him to their old village. By the time he left, he had over six hundred warriors, including some Kickapoos, Winne-bagos, and Potawatomis. Together with wives and children, there were about two thousand Indians who followed Black Hawk back across the Mississippi River.

Black Hawk's "Long March": the retreat through Illinois and Wisconsin. Dotted line indicates where the exact route remains unknown to this day.

The crossing was made on April 6, 1832, at Yellow Banks, near the mouth of the Iowa River. Then the large band turned north, toward Saukenuk. Keokuk, anxious to protect the peaceful portion of the tribe, sent word to the American authorities of Black Hawk's action. General Henry Atkinson, based at Jefferson Barracks below St. Louis, was ordered to prevent the Indians from returning to Saukenuk. He hastily gathered the available troops, put them aboard the steamboats *Enterprise* and *Chieftain,* and on April 8 sailed up the river to Fort Armstrong on Rock Island. They reached it on April 12. Black Hawk, in the meantime, had been intercepted by the Prophet, who told him about the arriving soldiers and suggested that the band pass by Saukenuk and go on to the Prophet's own village, farther up the Rock River. There they could wait until more warriors came from other tribes to help Black Hawk in case of an encounter with the troops.

Black Hawk accepted the invitation, and the band continued up the Rock River. They passed Fort Armstrong just as General Atkinson was debarking from the *Enterprise,* and he heard their defiant singing and the menacing beating of drums. Atkinson was worried. There were only a few men stationed at Fort Armstrong, and he had brought only 220 men from Jefferson Barracks. He hesitated to confront the Indians with so small a force. If Black Hawk refused to obey the order to keep out of Saukenuk, fighting might break out, and the large Indian band might easily win. Such a victory would be a calamity. It might encourage other Indians to join Black Hawk or to resist the removal policy, now being carried out in full force.

Atkinson decided to do nothing for the present. The next day, April 13, he wrote to Governor Reynolds describing the situation. He said it was dangerous, but did not ask for the help of the Illinois militia. Like most regular United States

Army officers, Atkinson disliked local volunteers and avoided using them if at all possible.

The next morning Keokuk arrived with a group of peaceful Sac and Fox to confer with Atkinson. Keokuk blamed the situation on the bad influence of the Prophet, and asked for one more chance to talk to Black Hawk's followers, to see if he could urge them to return to the west side of the Mississippi. Atkinson said angrily that if one white man were injured by Black Hawk's band, he would destroy them. He agreed, however, to wait a few more days. Another meeting was set for April 18.

For the last time Keokuk tried to reason with Black Hawk. But the stubborn old chief still refused to listen and refused even to attend the council on April 18. At that meeting, Keokuk demonstrated his good faith toward the Americans by surrendering three of the braves who had taken part in the killings at the Menominee camp. But there was no word or move on the part of Black Hawk. Atkinson sent messengers to explain that crossing the Mississippi had been a violation of the agreement signed by Black Hawk himself, and warned the Indians to return immediately to the west bank. Black Hawk's reply was to insult the messengers and repeat his refusal to leave the area. "We were determined never to be driven. . . ."

Atkinson, realizing that it was hopeless to expect Black Hawk's band to return quietly across the Mississippi, prepared for trouble. He drew up defense plans for the nearby garrisons, conferred with the agents of the neighboring tribes, and sent new ultimatums to Black Hawk. The Sac chief himself was not too disturbed by these preparations— "if he wished to *fight* us, he might come on!"—but the Winnebagos, near whose village the British Band was camped, grew uneasy. Soon Black Hawk realized that he had worn out his welcome and, even worse, that the Winnebagos had no intention of helping him fight, as the Prophet had promised. Feeling betrayed, Black Hawk moved his people away from the Winnebago village, going farther up the Rock River toward the country of the Potawatomis.

On the morning of April 28 the band reached Dixon's Ferry. Black Hawk told John Dixon that his aim was to settle quietly and raise corn on Potawatomi land, a few miles to the east. The band continued their journey till they reached the junction of the Rock and Kishwaukee rivers. There they met a delegation of Potawatomis, and Black Hawk received the worst news of all. Not only were the Potawatomis unwilling to join the British Band in any action against the United States, but they flatly informed the astonished Black Hawk that the British had no intention of helping, either. The Potawatomis added that they could not give Black Hawk's band any corn to supplement his own supplies, which were already alarmingly low. And finally the Potawatomis were not happy over the prospect of Black Hawk remaining near them. His presence meant trouble with the American troops, which the Potawatomis were anxious to avoid.

Black Hawk felt betrayed and abandoned. Without military aid, without new food supplies, with no invitation from any Indian village to remain as visitors, there was nothing to do but give way. Now he was ready to hold council with General Atkinson and return across the Mississippi.

But it was too late. Without the knowledge or deliberate intention of either Atkinson or Black Hawk, the machinery of war had already been started.

chapter eight

The Battle of Stillman's Run

When General Atkinson wrote to Governor Reynolds on April 13 to inform him of Black Hawk's return, he did not ask for military help, though later on he did suggest that a few ranger companies be held ready for further orders. But Reynolds, always prepared to explode at the slightest hint of "Indian troubles," reacted automatically and violently to the news. As soon as Atkinson's letter reached him, on April 16, he announced publicly that Black Hawk had seized the country around Rock Island and had placed the settlers in "eminent danger." Sixteen hundred militiamen were needed instantly, he continued, and if men did not "volunteer" to serve, they would be drafted.

114

The border settlers reacted to these pronouncements with alarm and panic. Some left the area immediately, moving back to the safer interior. Others abandoned their spring corn planting and hurried to volunteer. Among the volunteers in the little town of New Salem was Abraham Lincoln, at that time a clerk in Offut's general store. Lincoln, twenty-three years old, joined up not out of fear or pure patriotism, but for entirely personal reasons. He had become interested in politics and was running for a seat in the Illinois House of Representatives in the approaching elections. A term in the army would look good on his record. A second motive for enlisting was the imminent loss of his job. Denton Offut had been drinking heavily and neglecting the store. Business was falling off and might soon disappear altogether, taking young Lincoln's job with it. With a group of his friends, he signed up on April 21 for a term of thirty days.

Governor Reynolds had asked mainly for cavalry, so Lincoln borrowed a horse, having none of his own. He rode to Beardstown, where the volunteers had been asked to assemble. The men were divided into companies and told to choose their own captains. Lincoln and a man named Kirkpatrick were the leading candidates. Kirkpatrick was a sawmill owner who had once hired Lincoln to move some logs, but when the job was finished, Kirkpatrick paid him two dollars less than the agreed rate. Lincoln's friends were eager to show their disapproval of Kirkpatrick, though even the strangers in the small company had come to like Lincoln's friendly, joking manner in the few days they had been together. They were also impressed by his outstanding ability in wrestling, racing, and jumping. As Lincoln and Kirkpatrick stood side by side, each militiaman went and stood behind the one they wanted for captain. Twice as many stood behind Lincoln as behind Kirkpatrick.

Lincoln thereupon became the leader of the sixty-eight

men entered on the official register as "Captain Abraham
Lincoln's Company of the First Regiment of the Brigade of
Mounted Volunteers, commanded by Brigadier General
Samuel Whiteside." He made a little speech, thanking his
men for the "unexpected and undeserved" honor they had
bestowed upon him. Years later he said that this election as
captain was "a success which gave me more pleasure than
any I have had since."

Lincoln knew little about military routine or discipline;
his men knew even less and cared nothing at all about it.
They were rough, independent frontiersmen who resented
authority of any kind. The new captain's first order was
greeted by cries of "Go to hell!" But Lincoln's humor and
practical, common-sense approach to his men earned their
respect, so that he was able to handle them. His biggest
handicap was his own lack of military experience. The
five days of drilling at Beardstown, which constituted the
entire training period, taught him very little. Once, as he
was drilling his men, he had to get them through a gate. He
suddenly realized that he did not know the command that
would turn them endwise into a narrow line, so that they
could pass through the gate two by two. Just before they
reached it, he called out, "This company is dismissed for two
minutes, when it will fall in again on the other side of the
gate."

After five days of "training," the men set off for Yellow
Banks on the Mississippi River, where Black Hawk had
crossed over. Though Lincoln was able to manage his difficult company on the monotonous and uncomfortable
march, he got into trouble himself on two occasions. First, in
a moment of high spirits, he shot off his pistol, which was
against camp regulations; he was put under arrest for one
day. The second time, his men broke into the officers' quar-

ters and stole some whisky. The next morning some of them were too drunk to continue on the march. This time he was under arrest for two days. For the most part, however, he took his position seriously, keeping up the spirits of his men on tedious marches by telling them funny stories, and standing up for them against the regular army officers. There was a good deal of rivalry and jealousy between the regular and volunteer troops, with the regular army men generally getting favored treatment. The volunteers were so irritated by this that they threatened to rebel. Lincoln brought their complaints to the regular officers and warned of possible trouble. As a result, his men were given the same rations and treatment provided for the regular enlisted men.

Lincoln did no real fighting in the Black Hawk War, leaving before the major battles took place. He was to say later that the only blood drawn from him during that war was taken by mosquitoes. And far from killing any Indians, he saved the life of the only one with whom he came in contact. An old Indian wandered into the camp, and the soldiers ran up to kill him. They had enlisted to fight and kill Indians, and here was one conveniently at hand. Lincoln outran the men, leaped to the side of the Indian, who then showed his military pass, and prevented the men from harming the old native.

When the brief term of service was over his men went home, but Lincoln reenlisted for two additional terms as a scout. He left the army for good on July 10. On the way home his horse was stolen, and he had to go the rest of the way on foot and by canoe.

This short, superficial contact with the Black Hawk War was Lincoln's only experience of army life. Yet it provided him with a sympathetic understanding of the soldier's point of view and with a practical comprehension of the problems and hardships confronting the men in the field. It was this experience that he was able to draw upon as Commander in Chief of the Union Army during the Civil War.

It was in the middle of May, soon after Governor Reynolds had called up the militia, that Black Hawk decided to yield to American demands and return to the west bank of the Mississippi. By this time he knew that no one—neither the British in Canada nor any Indian tribe—would help him defy the American army. There was nothing left for him to do but notify General Atkinson of his decision to return and arrange for a safe passage across the river.

If Black Hawk's peace overture had been received in good faith, the "war" would have evaporated before it had a chance to start. But through the blundering of Governor Reynolds' militia, brought about by the even greater blundering of General Atkinson and the impatience of Reynolds himself, Black Hawk's peace message never got through.

Atkinson had put the regular troops—only 340 men— under the command of Colonel Zachary Taylor, whom the Sac and Fox had already met in battle. It was Taylor who had been sent to destroy Saukenuk and its inhabitants during the War of 1812. Perhaps he remembered that it was Black Hawk, together with a small detachment of British artillery, who had defeated him in that engagement.

The volunteer militia were led by General Samuel Whiteside. Atkinson ordered the 1500 mounted volunteers to proceed along the Rock River to the Prophet's village, near which Black Hawk was supposed to be camping. The regular troops, together with 165 unmounted volunteers, were sent by boat, along with supplies for the whole operation. Two keelboats and a few smaller vessels were used. Atkinson himself went with the boats. Since the mounted volunteers would reach the Prophet's village before the slower-moving boats could arrive, Atkinson gave Whiteside advance instructions. First, he was to determine how close to the village Black Hawk was. Then, if it was possible to make contact with the chief, Whiteside was to talk him into surrender or "coerce him to submission." If Black Hawk was not near the village, Whiteside was to wait until Atkinson arrived with the regular troops.

This deployment of troops and officers was unwise. Atkinson, though sharing the general army distrust of untrained and undisciplined volunteers, nevertheless sent them into a sensitive area ahead of the regulars. If he had to send the mounted militia by land, he should have accompanied them himself instead of going by boat. Or he could have given Whiteside instructions to wait for the boat's arrival before taking any action. Instead he left a strategic move to be executed by raw volunteers. Zachary Taylor said, a few months later, that there was "little doubt in my mind" that if the regular troops had reached Black Hawk first, or at least at the same time as the militia, the war would never have taken place.

As it was, when Whiteside reached the Prophet's village and discovered that Black Hawk had already left the region, he ignored the orders to wait there for Atkinson. He burned down most of the village, then continued up the Rock River after Black Hawk.

On May 14, Whiteside's volunteers reached Dixon's Ferry, named after John Dixon who, besides running the ferry that crossed the Rock River, maintained a store, bank, inn, and post office in his ninety-foot log house. He was the only white man in the area, and his establishment had become an unofficial army headquarters.

At Dixon's Ferry, Whiteside learned that Black Hawk was about twenty-five miles farther up the river. But the volunteers were too exhausted to continue. Heavy rains had made the going slow and difficult. Rations were low, and the only fresh supplies to be obtained were those being brought up by boat. Whiteside decided to wait for Atkinson before proceeding farther.

With him, however, was Governor Reynolds who had other ideas. Reynolds, present in his capacity as commander in chief of the Illinois militia, was eager for action against the Indians. Two ranger battalions, sent out earlier to patrol the area, were at Dixon's Ferry when Whiteside's party arrived. They were well rested and looking for excitement. To them, as to volunteers generally, the whole expedition was a lark; many had joined partly "for the sport of killing Indians." They begged Governor Reynolds to let them go on a scouting expedition after Black Hawk. The Governor readily agreed and ordered Major Isaiah Stillman, leader of one of the battalions, to take the fresh ranger troops, find the Indians, and "coerce them into submission."

Almost at this very moment General Atkinson, perhaps becoming aware of his error, decided to recall the militia. But in those days of slow communications, by the time Atkinson sat down to write the recall order and long before it had a chance to reach Whiteside, Stillman and his 275 volunteers caught up with their first Indians.

The volunteers had left Dixon's Ferry in the morning and by six o'clock were beginning to set up camp for the night. Still regarding the expedition as pure sport, the high-spirited rangers were behaving as though they were on a picnic.

Black Hawk, meanwhile, was taking part in a sad ceremonial feast. It was a farewell gesture to the Potawatomi delegation who had brought him the unhappy news about the nonexistence of British support and the inability of their own tribe to provide him with any corn. In the middle of the feast, Indian riders rushed in, saying that a large force of white soldiers were making camp only a few miles away.

Black Hawk, thinking that Atkinson was at the head of these troops, sent three braves with a message of surrender. The messengers were to escort the white leaders to Black Hawk, or if Atkinson preferred, Black Hawk would go to the American camp.

The three warriors set out carrying a white flag, a truce symbol scrupulously honored by almost every Indian tribe. After they left, Black Hawk decided to send five others, to observe from a distance what reception the three envoys would receive. The first three, bearing the flag, approached Stillman's camp and were immediately surrounded by a crowd of excited volunteers. Yelling and swearing, the volunteers pulled the three young Indians into camp and began hurling questions at them. Another volunteer caught sight of the second group of five braves, far off on the prairie. He shouted, and almost instantly whatever military discipline existed among the rangers disappeared. Men leaped on their horses, even upon those whose saddles had been removed for the night, and chased after the distant Indians who turned around and ran. The volunteers opened fire, killing two of the Indians. When the shots were heard back in the ranger camp, the remaining volunteers turned upon the three confused envoys. One was killed. The other two, one still holding the white flag, escaped and fled back to Black Hawk.

The old chief was enraged. His peace offer had been treated with dishonor and treachery. A large number of white soldiers, cheering jubilantly over their first kill, were still riding hard after the escaping Indians. Most of Black Hawk's band was camped several miles away. Less than fifty warriors had accompanied him to the feast. Gathering these around him, he tore the truce flag to pieces and urged his men to defend themselves bravely. Then he hid them behind some bushes and waited for the soldiers to come.

As the first riders approached, the Indians jumped out, uttering ferocious war whoops. The white soldiers, taken

completely by surprise, stampeded. They swerved around
and raced back even faster than they had come, pursued by
the yelling Indians. When they reached camp, they kept on
riding, slowing down briefly only to shout warnings to those
who had remained there. These men, unable to make out in
the increasing darkness just what was happening or how
many Indians were chasing the volunteers, leaped on their
own horses and went along with the rest, abandoning all
their equipment, which Black Hawk happily collected the
next morning.

The terrified rangers fled all the way back to Dixon's
Ferry. There they described a horrendous engagement with
at least a thousand Indians. The first arrivals, coming in the
middle of the night, thought they were the only survivors; to
the appalled Reynolds and Whiteside it looked as though
Stillman's entire force had been virtually wiped out. By the
next morning, however, all but fifty-two of the men had
come in, and during the next three days all but eleven would
turn up. However, in the agitated report sent that first night
by Governor Reynolds to General Atkinson, the event was
described as an overwhelming defeat by the Indians, who
were said to include not only Sac and Fox, but Potawatomis
and Winnebagos.

This premature report, together with the next morning's
account of fifty-two missing and believed dead, spread
through the frontier. More settlers fled to the interior or
joined together in quickly built forts. Reynolds called for additional volunteers, and Washington sent urgent orders to
General Atkinson to take more effective action against the
Indians. Even before the "Battle of Stillman's Run," as it
came to be called, President Jackson had become impatient
with Atkinson's failure to remove the Indians from the area.
Atkinson was now ordered to take all necessary steps and to
use whatever troops or volunteer militia he needed.

The Black Hawk War had become inevitable.

chapter nine

The Long March Begins

Lincoln and his company of volunteers arrived at Dixon's Ferry just after the debacle of Stillman's Run. A few days later their term of enlistment ended. The emergency, however, had entered a more acute stage, so that some volunteers—among them, Lincoln—reenlisted. Others were glad to leave, claiming they had to go home for the spring planting.

The mood of the volunteers had been sharply jolted. Stillman's rangers had thought they were in for a period of fun and frolic when they enlisted. They were going out to chase Indians. Instead the Indians had chased them, brandishing real tomahawks, in deadly seriousness. Now that the posi-

tions of the opponents appeared to be reversed, this was no
longer a game.

To the more exposed settlers, friction with Indians had
never seemed just a game. But now the fear and tension grew
worse than ever, heightened by several new Indian aggres-
sions. Most of these were committed by Potawatomis,
Winnebagos, or Kickapoos who had little or nothing to do
with Black Hawk's band. But, as usual, what one Indian or
tribe did was blamed on all Indians. At the moment blame
fell especially on the Sac and Fox.

Other tribes, though still unwilling to help Black Hawk,
had been so encouraged by his triumph over Stillman that
they engaged in a series of attacks on outlying settlers. The
worst of these occurred less than a week after Stillman's demoralized rangers rode into Dixon's Ferry with their exaggerated accounts of anywhere from one to two thousand
ferocious warriors scourging the area. On May 20 about
forty Indians, mostly Potawatomis but including three
young Sacs, attacked a farm on Indian Creek where several
white families were staying. The Potawatomis had had a
quarrel with the owner of the farm about a dam he had built
across the creek, insisting that it interfered with their fishing.
They killed, scalped, and mutilated fifteen people, including
women and children. Two young girls, Rachel and Sylvia
Hall, were carried off by the Sac warriors. Black Hawk said
later it was "to save their lives," but to the white community
it was kidnapping. The girls were brought to Black Hawk,
who soon turned them over to the Winnebagos for transfer to
the whites. Two weeks after their capture the girls were released.

While news of the Indian Creek massacre and kidnapping
was circulating among the horrified settlers, a war party of
thirty Winnebagos ran across seven white men carrying mes-
sages from General Atkinson. They killed four of them, in-

cluding the Rock Island agent, Felix St. Vrain. The Sac and Fox were blamed for these deaths, as well as for other Indian attacks or crimes occurring at the time.

The outcry, which had begun when Black Hawk first crossed the Mississippi and had risen sharply after Stillman's Run, reached a crescendo after the killings by the Potawatomis and Winnebagos. A St. Louis newspaper said the only atonement possible was to slaughter Indians in return, "The lives of a hundred Indians is too small for that of *each* of their fallen victims," while another newspaper editor called for a "war of extermination until there shall be no Indian (*with his scalp on*) left in the north part of Illinois."

The violation of his peace flag had made Black Hawk feel that he had no alternative but to stay and fight. He had expected the flag of truce to be observed and a council called to arrange the formalities of retreat. But "instead of this *honorable course* which *I* have always practised in war, I was *forced* into War. . . ."

His success at Stillman's Run was completely unexpected: he had been greatly outnumbered—almost three hundred soldiers against only forty braves—and totally unprepared for battle. In one sense it had been a dangerous victory for him, leading him to underestimate his enemy and to overrate his own military strength. The bold attacks by other tribes against white settlements encouraged him still further. He changed his mind about surrendering and, instead, committed himself to resistance. He did not, however, want to engage in another open battle immediately, knowing how badly outmatched he was by the whites. He decided that the best thing to do for the present was to retreat and find a safe place to hide the women and children in his band. To cover his retreat and to replenish his dwindling supplies, he sent out small raiding parties.

One of these forays was against a fort on the Apple River, near the lead mining town of Galena. The fort was one of several built by the local miners after the scares of Stillman's Run and the Indian Creek massacre. The miners, worried about their isolated location, had organized themselves into five companies of armed men, including one headed by Colonel Henry Dodge, a future governor of Wisconsin. The editor of the Galena newspaper asked his readers to show their courage by bringing in Indian scalps and dyeing their knives with human blood, preferably "from the heart of a Sac."

Black Hawk laid siege to the fort for twelve hours, killing two defenders and losing four of his own men. Unable to make headway he left, carrying off livestock and other badly needed supplies.

His original plan of retreat was to go to the headwaters of the Rock River. To throw his pursuers off the trail, he detoured east along the Kishwaukee River. There he met some Winnebagos who offered to guide him up into Wisconsin, to a place where they could hide in the marshes. The band turned north and began a long trek to the Four Lakes district of what is now Dane County, in central Wisconsin. This was the beginning of the famous march through Illinois and Wisconsin, with the United States Army trailing after the elusive Indians, in a frustrating, frazzling, now-you-see-them, now-you-don't game. But the developing situation was no game for the Indians.

chapter ten

Now You See Them, Now You Don't

While Black Hawk's band was disappearing into the marshes of the Wisconsin lake district, the white settlers, the United States Army, and Keokuk's peaceful followers were all left in a state of confusion and distress.

After the Battle of Stillman's Run, no one knew exactly where Black Hawk and his people were. There were wild rumors, fortified by the sudden forays of war parties from other tribes. The settlers believed these raids were all the work of Black Hawk. Stories were circulated that he planned to attack first one place, then another. In the general panic more and more settlers abandoned their farms.

One family, living near a riverbank, fled across the river

with their eleven children. The father had to carry the children across the dangerously high waters one at a time. When he thought they were all over, he heard a cry from the other side. Hastily checking, he discovered that he had brought over only ten of the children. Though he was exhausted, he turned toward the torrent once more. "Never mind Susan," cried his wife. Getting ten over was more than they had expected, she said, "and we can better spare Susan than you, my dear." The family then continued their flight. This was a common attitude—and actual experience—on the frontier. Fortunately for this particular Susan, aged four, she was found by a neighbor and safely returned to her family later on.

General Atkinson, in the meantime, had called up reinforcements of regular troops, bringing their number to four hundred, and asked for three thousand more volunteers. He also enlisted a few hundred friendly Indians to serve as auxiliaries. Keokuk volunteered to serve, to prove that he and his followers had nothing to do with Black Hawk's hostile actions. Earlier, Keokuk's band had entertained the volunteers at Yellow Banks with a war dance. Other Indians, however, were incensed at Keokuk for turning against his own tribesmen, and he withdrew to an uncomfortable neutrality.

After the reinforcements arrived, General Atkinson set out in pursuit of Black Hawk. For three weeks patrols went out, searching for Black Hawk with little success. There were a few minor encounters between the Illinois militia and small groups of Indians, with the militia coming off badly in all but one engagement. Colonel Henry Dodge and his company of Galena miners heard that some Indians had been sighted on the Pecatonica River. On the morning of June 14, Dodge and twenty-nine men went after them and found eleven Indians hiding under a six-foot bank of earth. The Indians fired first, wounding three men. The rest of Dodge's miners immediately charged and, after a brief but violent struggle, killed and scalped every one of the Indians.

This small victory was a great boost to the sagging morale of the other volunteers. The settlers were also encouraged, though on the whole they took a dim view of the militia. Local farmers complained that the volunteers were doing as much damage to their poultry and hogs as to the Indians.

Another skirmish, with honors to the Indians this time, took place between Major John Dement and Black Hawk himself on June 25, at what was called the Battle of Kellogg's Grove, though it was in no sense a real battle. Atkinson, hearing from some Potawatomis and Winnebagos that Black Hawk was somewhere around Lake Koshkonong in Wisconsin, sent a battalion under Major Dement in that direction. On the way Dement was surprised by Black Hawk and a large number of warriors returning from the raid against the miners' fort on Apple River. Dement urged his men to stand and fight, but seeing themselves outnumbered by the Indians, most of the men retreated, leaving Dement and a few others alone on the field. Soon they, too, left. Black Hawk, always ready to admire the virtues of his enemies, said later about Dement: "This young chief deserves great praise for his courage and bravery; but, fortunately for us, his army was not all composed of such brave men!"

For the most part, Atkinson accomplished nothing, though by this time he was pursuing Black Hawk with a force of four hundred regulars, three thousand militiamen, and several hundred Indian auxiliaries. After the encounter at Kellogg's Grove, Black Hawk vanished again. Atkinson followed his trail up the Rock and Kishwaukee Rivers. On July 1, the troops reached Turtle Village, a Winnebago settlement on the border of Wisconsin and Illinois. They found the village deserted, but with traces showing that Black

Hawk's band had camped nearby. On July 3, Atkinson's scouts reported finding the main trail of the elusive Indians, and the force moved on to a spot just below Lake Koshkonong, which was really part of the Rock River. Atkinson sent out more scouts, but all they could find was one old, blind Sac. Under threats of death from Atkinson, the unhappy Indian provided the information that Black Hawk had moved up the left bank of the lake. The old Sac was later allowed to leave. He was assured that he would be unharmed, but some volunteers caught and killed him, taking his scalp as a souvenir.

For two days patrols searched through the swamps in the direction pointed out by the old man but found nothing. By this time supplies were running out, forcing Atkinson to stop further pursuit for the present. The inexperienced volunteers had wasted their rations and were going hungry. In an effort to stretch out the remaining food, Atkinson dismissed all but two of the Indian auxiliaries. He sent three brigades of white soldiers to Fort Hamilton and Fort Winnebago for fresh supplies. Colonel Dodge and his company were sent to Fort Winnebago for the same purpose. The remaining men began to build Fort Koshkonong, at the mouth of the Scuppernong River.

Black Hawk's trail had disappeared in the swampy ground, leaving Atkinson's army nothing to fight but mud and mosquitoes. Many of the dispirited volunteers left, feeling that with the campaign bogged down, their services were no longer needed. Among those departing were Governor Reynolds and Abraham Lincoln, who had just completed his third term of service. Atkinson was left with the remnant, miserable and discouraged, seeing his whole career threatened simply because, with almost four thousand men under his command, he could not find a few hundred wretched, badly supplied Indian braves.

In Washington President Andrew Jackson was indignant. It seemed inconceivable to the old Indian fighter that a large and powerful white army could not seek out and destroy one small fraction of an Indian tribe. He instructed John Robb, acting Secretary of War, to reprimand Atkinson: "I am directed by the President to say that he views with utter astonishment and deep regret, this state of things. . . ."

Atkinson's failure was not only irritating to Jackson, it was becoming politically dangerous as well. Jackson's great popularity at this time rested partly on his success in making Indian lands available and safe for white settlers. A new election was coming up, and Jackson, running for reelection, could not afford to provide his opponents with ammunition against him. By the end of May the pursuit of Black Hawk had already cost $150,000, and another $150,000 had been requested for a war that was going badly.

To General Jackson, veteran of so many victorious battles against the Indians, it appeared that large-scale, decisive military action was now called for. On June 15 he put Major General Winfield Scott in charge of the whole operation, over General Atkinson himself. Scott was a bold, adventurous soldier whose rank had been raised after his successes in the War of 1812. He was to go on to even greater triumphs in the Mexican War, when he would be supreme commander of the army, and run for President against Franklin Pierce in 1852.

Jackson ordered Scott to assemble a large force in Chicago and then to pin down Black Hawk between that force and Atkinson's. Scott was authorized to use eight hundred regular army men, six ranger companies, and as many volunteers as he might need.

He began to gather his men immediately, taking nine companies from the Great Lakes army posts and nine artillery companies from Forts Monroe and McHenry and from

New York harbor. Two additional companies of infantry were sent from Baton Rouge, Louisiana, up the Mississippi directly to General Atkinson's position.

Scott's men proceeded to Buffalo and then on to Chicago by way of the Great Lakes. The world-wide epidemic of cholera, which had been carried to Canada early in 1832, had just begun to spread down into the United States. Someone brought the infection on board one of the steamboats carrying the men, and it spread rapidly and disastrously through the entire force. Some of the worst cases had to be left at ports along the way, while the rest reached Chicago on July 10 in very poor shape. A great many men died or were unable to continue, and Scott hesitated to take the remainder to join Atkinson. If there was still any infection among them, as seemed quite possible, the cholera would spread to Atkinson's men, and then the war would really be lost. He decided to remain in Chicago for a while longer, and sent instructions to Atkinson to continue the war on his own.

The Indians were having their own troubles. Supplies had dwindled, and it became increasingly hard to find new sources of food. As long as they had been near Lake Koshkonong, the Indians were able to fish for bass, pike, and catfish. But when they left Koshkonong to go to the Four Lakes, there was no more fish to be had, and the small game was too scarce to provide enough food. The situation became critical once they set up camp in the country around the Four Lakes of "Ouisconsin," the area that now contains the city of Madison. They had selected the spot as a hiding place because the marshy approach would make it difficult for their enemies to track them down or, if they did, to attack easily. But the very conditions that made it good for hiding also made it poor for camping. There was little fish or game to be found in the swamps, and it was too far from any settlements to make raiding practical.

They were reduced to chewing on roots and the bark of trees. Some of the horses had to be killed and used for meat. Older people, unable to take such hardship, began to die of starvation and exhaustion. The children also suffered, and cried from hunger. The Winnebago, Potawatomi, and Kickapoo braves who had joined Black Hawk in the early days, when his venture had promised excitement and the hope of retaliation against the whites, left him now to return to the comfort of their own tribes. Their departure seriously cut down the number of warriors in the band.

Black Hawk watched the old people weaken and listened to the weeping of the hungry children and women, and felt that he could not subject them to any further rigors of a war with the Americans. When he heard that Atkinson was following with a large force, he began to worry. The general might surround the camp and crush the band inside it.

Once again Black Hawk decided to yield. He would break camp immediately, before Atkinson could encircle it, and lead his people back across the Mississippi into Iowa, where they could join Keokuk and the main portion of the tribe. He had tried to regain Saukenuk and failed. There was nothing more he could do.

His plan was to try to elude the American army, lead his band west to the Wisconsin River, guided by five Winnebagos who knew the country, then descend the Wisconsin to the Mississippi and cross that river into Iowa.

If Black Hawk had been permitted to carry out his plan, a good deal of bloodshed would have been avoided, and the war again have ended almost before it began. But Atkinson had no way of knowing what was in the chief's mind, and Black Hawk, having been betrayed once by the violation of his flag of truce, had no intention of laying himself open to such treachery again.

Unfortunately, just as Black Hawk was preparing to leave the Four Lakes, Colonel Dodge and his volunteer company of miners reached Fort Winnebago, due north of the Lakes. Dodge had been sent by Atkinson with instructions to get supplies from the fort and rejoin the main army as soon as possible. Dodge's men, however, had found the trail from Koshkonong to Winnebago rough going and refused to return by the same route. Before Dodge could decide just what to do, the Winnebago subagent of the area came to him and said he knew where Black Hawk was hiding. Disregarding Atkinson's instructions to return immediately, Dodge decided to go after Black Hawk. Even if he did not find the Indian band, at least it would provide a different return route for his complaining miners.

Accompanying Dodge and acting under his command was General James D. Henry's brigade. They had also been sent for supplies by Atkinson and had reached Fort Winnebago the day after Dodge. The combined forces took along an interpreter, Pierre Pacquette, half French and half Winnebago, and several Winnebago tribesmen to act as guides.

On July 18, they came across unmistakable traces of Black Hawk. Leaving their supply wagons behind, the men set off eagerly after the Indians. Three days later they found their first Indian, mourning beside the grave of his wife, who had died of starvation. They killed and scalped him before continuing. They encountered a few more Indians, half-starved and sick old men unable to keep up with the main band. These, too, were killed and scalped.

When Black Hawk started for the Wisconsin River, he had placed twenty warriors led by Neapope at the rear of the band, to watch for signs of the pursuing enemy. Dodge's advance scouts caught up with this rear guard, and a few skirmishes took place during which two braves were killed.

The main body of white soldiers rushed after the band and reached it just as the Indians were preparing to cross the

Wisconsin River some twenty miles below Fort Winnebago. If Black Hawk had been alone with his warriors under normal circumstances, he would not have been caught in this way, but the presence of women and children and the weakness of their half-starved ponies had slowed him down. Nor would he have engaged in battle in such an unstrategic location and against such odds. Now, however, he was forced to stand and fight, in order to give the women and children time to escape across the river.

He directed part of his men to help the women across as quickly as possible. Then, with a group of only fifty warriors, he faced the six hundred white attackers.

chapter eleven

The Battle of
Wisconsin Heights

The crossing of the Wisconsin River by the Indian women and children was a cleverly planned and executed maneuver. While the warriors held off the soldiers, the squaws hastily tore off strips of elm bark and tied them together at the ends to form makeshift canoes. Others made crude rafts, using mats and skins. Mothers floated their babies on pieces of bark torn from trees. Those who had ponies piled them with supplies and swam them across.

When all the women had embarked upon the river, half the warriors assigned to help them jumped into the water, lifting their guns clear with one arm and swimming with the other. The remaining braves continued to hold off the troops. The swimmers went to an island in the middle of the river, taking cover as soon as they reached it. Then they began shooting at the white soldiers while, protected by their fire, the second group of warriors swam over. A young lieutenant, Jefferson Davis, described it as a "brilliant exhibition of military tactics . . . a feat of the most consummate management and bravery, in the face of an enemy of greatly superior numbers. . . . Had it been performed by white men, it would have been immortalized as one of the most splendid achievements in military history."

Black Hawk called out his orders from the top of a small hill, sitting on a white pony. The American troops were on a flat piece of ground facing the river, while Black Hawk and the rest of his men were on the hills above them. For a short time they were able to fire down into the American position, but they were too greatly outnumbered to hold this advantage long. The Americans soon climbed the hill and drove the Indians down into a ravine. The firing continued until almost seven o'clock, when Dodge and Henry decided to stop. Their men were tired after the long march through the swampy land. It had rained almost all afternoon, and many of the flintlocks on the guns had become damp. Dodge and Henry agreed to let the men rest overnight and continue the battle in the morning.

They woke up to discover that Black Hawk and his warriors had crossed the river during the night. By this time, the troops had only one day's rations left, so Dodge and Henry decided against crossing the river after Black Hawk. If they had, they almost certainly would have caught up with him. Instead they spent the day resting and drying out and cleaning their equipment.

Early the next morning, about an hour and a half before dawn, the camp was awakened by the sound of someone speaking loudly in an Indian language. Pacquette and the

other Winnebagos had left right after the battle the day before, and there was no one in camp who could understand
what was being said. The voice of the unseen speaker continued for a while and then stopped abruptly.

Weeks later it was discovered that the voice was that of
Neapope, who had come with a message of surrender. He
had spoken in Winnebago, thinking that Pacquette or at
least some Winnebago guides would be in the camp. He had
talked about the miseries of the women and children, and
asked that Black Hawk and his people be permitted to go
back to the west bank of the Mississippi without interference
from the American soldiers. He promised that they would
remain across the river in peace and make no further attempt to return to their old homes.

But there was no one to understand or reply. After waiting
for some time in silence, Neapope left, and another chance
to stop the war was lost.

After the battle Black Hawk had been astonished when no
immediate effort was made to pursue him. His men formed
crude rafts and canoes out of bark hastily stripped from the
surrounding elm trees and crossed the Wisconsin to the farther shore, where the rest of the band was waiting.

At this point some of the Indians, mainly women, children, and old men, left the band to float down the Wisconsin
and try to reach the Mississippi on their own. They felt that
white soldiers would not molest such obvious noncomba-
tants. "I had no objection to their leaving me," said Black
Hawk, "as my people were all in a desperate condition—
being worn out with travelling, and starving from hunger."
In fact, he hoped the departing group would carry his offer
of surrender to Fort Crawford at Prairie du Chien, where the
Wisconsin flows into the Mississippi.

But when the raft containing the miserable, half-starved,

unarmed Indians approached Fort Crawford, they were fired upon. The commander of the fort had been alerted by Colonel Dodge to watch for any of Black Hawk's band who might try to escape by that route. There was no chance to beg for permission to cross the Mississippi or to convey Black Hawk's offer of surrender. Many were killed, either by gunshot or drowning. Some were taken prisoner. Others managed to escape into the woods, where they died of starvation or were sought out and killed by a group of Menominees and Winnebagos who were serving as United States Army auxiliaries under a white officer, Colonel Samuel Stambaugh. Using torches to light up the woods, the auxiliaries hunted down the survivors and killed or took them prisoner. There were thirty-four captives, in such an appalling state—famished, exhausted, dressed in rags—that the Winnebagos begged the whites to help them. In a sudden reversal of attitude, the government supplied them with food and clothing.

While this group was going down the Wisconsin River, the rest of the band under Black Hawk headed west, walking overland toward the Mississippi. Some Winnebagos, relatives of the Prophet, went along to show them the way. The going was very slow. The Indians were weak from hunger and privation, and there were few horses left. Some had been eaten as a desperate measure against starvation; others had been killed during the battle. Many old people, wounded warriors, and young children died. By the time the band reached the Mississippi on August 1, there were only about five hundred left out of the original two thousand who had followed Black Hawk so hopefully.

They reached the Mississippi a short distance below the place where the Bad Axe River flows into it. Black Hawk felt it would be impossible for the entire band to cross the river before the white army caught up with them. He knew the soldiers were following and were moving much more rapidly than the hunger-weakened Indians encumbered by women, children, old people, and the sick and wounded.

He called a council to discuss the problem. Black Hawk himself was in favor of turning north into Winnebago country, and trying to hide by mingling with that tribe. But his band refused. They had had enough of running and hiding. Safety and rest lay on the shore which they could see across the river, and across the river they insisted upon going.

Once again they began to construct makeshift rafts and canoes, working as fast as their exhausted condition would allow. A few did manage to get across, some by swimming the last part of the way after their inadequate rafts collapsed or turned over. One large raft capsized, and most of the women and children on it drowned in the dangerous waters of the Mississippi.

Suddenly a steamboat, the *Warrior,* appeared. It was coming downstream from a trip to Minnesota. The vessel carried a detachment of twenty-one soldiers under the command of Lieutenant James W. Kingsbury, who had been sent to ask Chief Wabashaw of the Sioux to watch out for Black Hawk and intercept him. The Sioux, old enemies of the Sac and Fox, had agreed to send a hundred and fifty warriors to patrol the shores of the Mississippi. The *Warrior,* now returning from this mission, also carried an artillery piece, a six-pounder.

When the vessel came in sight, the Indians were terrified, but Black Hawk reassured them. He knew the captain, Joseph Throckmorton, and said he would make another attempt to surrender. He hoped to save the lives of at least the women and children. As reported by one of the braves later, Black Hawk said, " 'I will go on board that boat.' He told the men to put down their guns, and the women got behind trees." Then, added Black Hawk in his own description of the incident, "I took a small piece of white cotton, and put it on a pole, and called to the captain of the boat, and told him to send his little canoe ashore, and let me come on board. The people on the boat asked whether we were Sacs or Winnebagos. I told a Winnebago to tell them that we were Sacs, and wanted to give ourselves up! A Winnebago on the boat called to us *'to run and hide, that the whites were going to shoot!'* "

Like all his earlier attempts to surrender, this one, too, was unsuccessful. Just as at Stillman's Run, the white flag, international symbol of surrender, was not honored. But this time it was as much the result of misunderstanding as of outright rejection. The Winnebago interpreter misunderstood Black Hawk and told Lieutenant Kingsbury that the Indians wanted the whites to come ashore. Kingsbury refused and said that two natives should come aboard. Black Hawk was confused by the reply and remained silent while he thought about it. Kingsbury had been suspicious of the truce flag from the beginning, believing it was a trick to draw his men into ambush. He misunderstood the silence and thought the Indians were trying to gain time while preparing to attack. He ordered the six-pounder to fire three quick rounds directly at the natives on shore. Many were killed instantly. The others, after the first paralyzing shock, seized their guns, ran behind trees, and began shooting back. The gunfire continued back and forth for about two hours. Then the *Warrior* ran low on fuel, pulled up anchor, and sailed down to Prairie du Chien to get wood. Twenty-three Indians had been killed, one white man wounded.

Again Black Hawk proposed that they flee north, this time to seek refuge among the Chippewa, instead of trying to cross the Mississippi. He was afraid the *Warrior* would soon be back. Even worse, he expected the troops who had been pursuing them overland to arrive at any moment. But only

fifty members of the band agreed with his reasoning and left
with him that night. The Winnebago Prophet, who had accompanied the band on this last march, went with Black
Hawk.

The rest stubbornly persisted in trying to escape over the
river. A few succeeded in getting over during the night, but
most of them decided to wait until dawn. Before the sun rose,
however, General Atkinson arrived as Black Hawk had
feared, and the last disastrous engagement of the war took
place.

chapter twelve

The Bad Axe Massacre

If Colonel Dodge and General Henry had crossed the Wisconsin River after the Battle of Wisconsin Heights, they would have caught up with Black Hawk's slowly moving band in no time at all. But they had left their supplies behind in order to pursue the Indians as far as the river, and they now decided to rejoin Atkinson, following their original instructions. They marched to the fort at Blue Mounds, Wisconsin, about twenty miles to the south. Late the next day, Atkinson arrived there from Lake Koshkonong.

It had been an exceedingly uncomfortable march, and Atkinson's men were exhausted and discouraged. General Scott and his troops were still detained by cholera in Chicago. The news brought by Dodge and Henry that they had at last made contact with the enemy and that apparently Black Hawk's warriors were also weakened and discouraged provided some comfort, but Atkinson was still worried. His entire future might depend upon the outcome of this irritating little war, and he had yet to reach the Indians, pursuing them through difficult and completely unknown country.

Atkinson's purpose was no longer simply to drive Black Hawk back over the Mississippi. His latest orders from Washington were to punish the stubborn Indians. President Jackson explicitly demanded that Black Hawk be taken prisoner and an example made of him. The office of the Secretary of War issued a statement saying that "Black Hawk & his party must be chastized and a speedy & honorable termination put to this war, which will hereafter deter others from the like unprovoked hostilities by Indians on our frontier."

This time, Atkinson felt, he *must* find Black Hawk and put an end to the whole affair. With thirteen hundred carefully picked men and rations for eight days, he marched to the Wisconsin River and was across it by July 28, more than five days later than Black Hawk. After searching for less than four miles, Atkinson's scouts picked up the trail of the retreating Indians. The morale of the troops lifted noticeably, though the country through which the trail led was no less difficult than before. Instead of the marshy terrain which they had crossed between the Rock River and the Wisconsin Lakes, they now had to cope with very hilly and heavily forested country. The tangled underbrush made progress hard, especially for those on horseback. These were mostly the volunteers, while the infantry consisted of regular army men. There was little grass, which presented a problem in feeding the horses. Saplings had to be cut to provide their food. The wagon holding medical supplies could not manage the rough ground and had to be left behind.

All this would have greatly discouraged the troops had it not been for increasing traces of Black Hawk, traces which clearly showed that the condition of the Indians was becoming steadily worse. Valuable equipment—traps, blankets, cooking utensils—had been dropped, revealing the desperate haste of the fleeing band. The bodies of Indians who had died of wounds or obvious starvation began to appear. They found one living brave, who had grown too weak to keep up with the rest. The most important indication of Indian weakness was the fact that no rearguard delaying actions were being fought, according to the usual custom in covering a retreat.

By the time Black Hawk's band reached the Mississippi, Atkinson was only twenty miles behind. On the night of August 2, after the *Warrior* incident, the troops made camp at around eight o'clock in the evening. After four hours of rest, they went forward again and came upon the Indians in the early hours of the morning. The Indians were caught unprepared. They managed to return the first fire but were quickly surrounded and overwhelmed by the soldiers. The encounter turned into a massacre. Women and children, screaming with fear, were shot or clubbed to death along with the braves. Some who rushed into the water in panic were drowned. Yells, screams, war whoops, and the piercing tones of a bugle formed a shattering accompaniment to the terrible scene. A brave who managed to escape told Black Hawk that the Indians had tried to surrender but "the whites paid no attention to their entreaties—but commenced *slaughtering* them!"

A few of the warriors managed to swim out to some small islands in the river where they hid in the trees. But just then the *Warrior* appeared again, returning from Prairie du Chien. Atkinson ordered a number of companies to board the boat and attack the islands. The assault began with several rounds from the *Warrior*'s cannon. Then the troops landed, forced the surviving Indians out of the trees and into the river, where soldiers stationed along the banks shot them. Those who were not killed by cannon or gunfire died by drowning. One white observer later wrote: "The Indians were pushed literally into the Mississippi, the current of which was at one time perceptibly tinged with the blood of the Indians who were shot on its margin & in the stream."

The shooting continued for eight hours. Terrified women and children, crouching behind bushes or in the tall grass, were killed as the white soldiers shot at any possible hiding places. After the battle, many soldiers expressed regret for killing these helpless innocents, claiming it was unintentional, since it was impossible to tell just who might be concealed behind a bush. General Winfield Scott later apologized directly to the Indians for the slaughter of their women and children, saying: "Some of them . . . were in the bushes and high grass, with their warriors, and were hurt or killed unavoidably, infinitely to the regret of our warriors."

Whether or not the killing was unavoidable, at least 150 dead Indians were found on the spot. Thirty-nine women and children were taken prisoner. The hundred or so who had managed to cross the river before Atkinson's arrival struggled on toward Keokuk's village. But about a week later they were cut off by Chief Wabashaw's Sioux band patrolling the farther shore under instructions from Atkinson. The Sioux killed sixty-eight, taking twenty-two women and children captive. By now only a handful of Black Hawk's band remained alive, and most of these were eventually captured.

Some of the survivors had escaped overland, and there were still Black Hawk and the fifty who had gone with him to be found. But Atkinson decided not to hunt them down at the moment. His men were worn out. Besides, he had just learned that General Scott had arrived at last to take over his command.

He sent his wounded men and the Indian captives to Prairie du Chien on the *Warrior*. Two days later the volunteers of the Illinois militia began their march to Fort Crawford and the end of their army service. Then Atkinson set out to turn over his command to General Scott. His last official act before doing so was to post a reward of one hundred dollars and twenty horses for the capture of Black Hawk and the other Indian leaders of the war.

chapter thirteen

Capture of Black Hawk

Before the Battle of the Bad Axe, Black Hawk had warned the band of what might happen and urged them to go north with him, to hide from the pursuing army. Those who remained did so out of their own free choice. Nevertheless, the survivors of that disaster blamed Black Hawk for deserting his people. "None of us liked the Prophet and Black Hawk leaving as they did," said one of them. "We said 'now they have brought us to ruin and lost us our women and children, then have run to save their own lives.'"

This judgment might seem unfair in view of the band's voluntary decision to remain. But years later, the great Chief Joseph of the Nez Percé and his brother, Chief Ollokot, found themselves in a similar situation. They were strongly opposed to their tribe's decision to fight rather than go to a reservation, but once the majority chose to fight, the brother chiefs felt it their duty to stay with their people and lead them in what they realized would be a futile struggle. This was in accord with Indian conceptions of responsibility; in that light there might be some justification for the complaint against Black Hawk.

Black Hawk himself had not felt it necessary to remain, once the band rejected his advice. But when a brave, who had escaped by hiding under the riverbank, brought him the "sorrowful news" from the Bad Axe, Black Hawk decided to give himself up. "I intended to give myself up to the American war chief, and *die,* if the Great Spirit saw proper!" First, however, he went to a Winnebago village at Prairie La Crosse, where he could have a white deerskin outfit made, in order to be properly dressed when he made his formal surrender to the whites.

General Scott, having no way of knowing that Black Hawk had resolved to give himself up, was making every effort to capture the missing leaders of the band. Rewards had been offered by Atkinson for their capture, and Scott renewed the offer. The first to be brought was Neapope, turned in with several other fugitives by Keokuk. The most important leaders, Black Hawk and the Winnebago Prophet, seemed to have disappeared, leaving nothing but rumors behind them. It was said that Black Hawk had escaped to Canada, that he was dead, that he had been seen at various points in Wisconsin or along the Mississippi.

The Winnebago were in trouble with the United States government because many of their people had helped Black Hawk. To demonstrate the good intentions of the tribe— and perhaps to collect the reward as well—a group of

Winnebagos went after Black Hawk. They found him near the Wisconsin Dells. After two days of close surveillance, they entered the camp at night when everyone was asleep and seized Black Hawk and the rest of his party. The fugitives surrendered quietly. They were through with resistance.

They were taken to Fort Crawford at Prairie du Chien, and handed over to Colonel Zachary Taylor. Taylor put Black Hawk and his two sons, and the Prophet and his son in the charge of young Lieutenant Jefferson Davis. Davis, who was to marry Taylor's daughter several years later, had graduated from West Point in 1828 and had been sent to Wisconsin for his first army service. Early in 1832 the frontier seemed fairly quiet; Black Hawk had not yet crossed the Mississippi. Davis, by that time in command of his company, was given a furlough from March to the end of July to attend to some personal affairs in Mississippi. After his return to Fort Crawford he was sent out with a small detachment to look for Black Hawk, but the Winnebagos caught the old chief first.

Davis's sympathies were all with Black Hawk. He believed that the white settlers had moved into Saukenuk prematurely and illegally, since the land had not yet been officially put up for sale. He felt that Black Hawk was right to protest. The war, said Davis later, might have been "averted by foresight and a little timely generosity on the part of the Government." He felt, too, that Atkinson had badly bungled the conduct of the war and that "the real heroes were Black Hawk and his savages."

When Davis left Fort Crawford at the end of March, the panic caused by Black Hawk's return to the east bank had not begun. If it had, Davis's leave would most likely have been canceled. In that case the two young men, twenty-three-year-old Abraham Lincoln and twenty-four-year old Jefferson Davis, who were later to lead the divided halves of their nation against each other, might have had their first encounter. But by the time Davis returned, Lincoln had already left. In the Civil War it would be Lincoln who would express his great concern for an enslaved minority. In the Black Hawk War, however, it was Davis who declared his sympathy with the harassed minority nation of Indians.

The Black Hawk War was filled with Presidents-to-be, Presidential hopefuls, governors, and other public office holders of the future. Besides Abraham Lincoln and Jefferson Davis, there were Zachary Taylor—Old Rough and Ready—who would become President in 1848, and General Winfield Scott, who would run for President on the Whig ticket in 1852. In addition to Governor John Reynolds, there were Thomas Ford, Thomas Carlin, and Joseph Duncan, all to become governors of Illinois. Colonel Henry Dodge would become governor of Wisconsin, and Orville H. Browning, a personal friend of Lincoln's, would become senator from Illinois and Secretary of the Interior.

Davis was present when Black Hawk, beautifully dressed in his new suit of white deerskin, and the other prisoners were brought to Colonel Taylor at Fort Crawford. Davis was especially aware of the old chief's "restless black eyes" beneath the scant eyebrows. The Roman nose and high forehead, together with his air of dignity, added to the impressive effect.

The Winnebagos were unhappy about their role in the capture of Black Hawk's party. One of them said, "My father, we deliver these men into your hands. . . . If they are to be hurt, we do not wish to see it. Wait until we are gone before it is done."

But there was no intention of hurting the defeated men.

Black Hawk, with some forty others, was put on the steamboat *Winnebago* in the custody of Jefferson Davis, who was to
deliver them to General Scott at Fort Armstrong. Davis
treated Black Hawk with all the courtesy and respect to
which a defeated military leader was entitled. Black Hawk
wrote warmly of Davis, calling him the "young war chief,
who treated us all with much kindness. He is a good and
brave young chief, with whose conduct I was much pleased.
On our way down we called at Galena, and remained a short
time. The people crowded to the boat to see us; but the war
chief would not permit them to enter the apartment where
we were—knowing from what his own feelings would have
been, if he had been placed in a similar situation, that we did
not wish to have a gaping crowd around us."

When they reached Fort Armstrong on Rock Island, they
found that the epidemic of cholera, which had delayed Scott
in Chicago, had hit Rock Island in full force. Davis was
ordered to continue down the river and take his prisoners to
Jefferson Barracks below St. Louis. As they paused briefly at
Rock Island, General Scott wanted to come on board to get a
close look at Black Hawk, the Winnebago Prophet, and the
other leaders of the troublesome little war. He came out in a
small boat, but the steamship's captain refused to allow him
aboard because of the danger of cholera contagion. Black
Hawk was disappointed. He said he had important things to
tell General Scott and probably regarded their meeting as a
confrontation of two important warlords. He thought the
captain was excessively anxious and that it was "absurd to
think that any of the people on the steam boat could be
afraid of catching the disease from a *well* man. But these
people have not got bravery like war chiefs, who never *fear*
any thing!"

Shortly afterward, two of the Indian prisoners came down
with cholera. Davis did what he could to relieve their suffer-

ing, but he also worried about the possible spread of the disease among the rest of the passengers. The sick Indians solved his problem by asking to be put ashore. The steamboat drew up close to the bank, and the two men got off. Davis said later that his "heart ached" when he saw the Indian who was suffering least support the head of his dying friend.

On the way to St. Louis, Black Hawk "surveyed the country that had cost us so much trouble, anxiety and blood, and that now caused me to be a prisoner of war. I reflected upon the ingratitude of the whites, when I saw their fine houses, rich harvests, and every thing desirable around them; and recollected that all this land had been ours, for which [I] and my people had never received a dollar, and that the whites were not satisfied until they took our village and our grave-yards from us, and removed us across the Mississippi."

When they reached Jefferson Barracks, the prisoners were turned over to Atkinson, whom the Indians called the White Beaver. He "received us kindly and treated us well." But soon Atkinson ordered the prisoners to be put in chains, to the humiliation of the proud old chief. "We were now confined to the barracks, and forced to wear the *ball and chain!* This was extremely mortifying, and altogether useless. Was the White Beaver afraid that I would break out of his barracks, and run away? . . . If I had taken him prisoner on the field of battle, I would not have wounded his feelings so much, by such treatment—knowing that a brave war chief would prefer *death* to *dishonor!* But I do not blame the White Beaver. . . . it is the custom among white soldiers, and, I suppose, was a part of his duty."

Aside from the shackles, Atkinson did everything to make him comfortable, as Black Hawk readily admitted. But, he added, such confinement was torture to an Indian, accustomed to "roam the forests" in unrestrained freedom.

This unrestrained freedom had been the core of Indian life, but Black Hawk acknowledged at last what Keokuk had seen all along: the arrival of the white man was putting an end to the traditional life and unlimited freedom of the Indian, and there was nothing the Indian could do about it. All the courageous resistance in the world was futile against the overwhelming strength and numbers of the whites. They would continue to spread, "like grease on a buffalo hide," and all the Indians could do was to try to extract from them a few safe havens where they might survive the danger of total disappearance as a race.

chapter fourteen

The Peace Treaty

While Black Hawk, Neapope, and the Prophet remained in humiliating confinement, Keokuk, faced with no further opposition from his rival, dealt with the peace negotiations and the inevitable loss of land. The war had been fought by Black Hawk and his band against the urgings of the rest of the tribe. Nevertheless, as customary in Indian-white relations, the entire tribe would have to pay for the peace, and it was Keokuk alone who now spoke for the Sac and Fox.

On the American side, General Scott was authorized to handle the negotiations, assisted by Governor Reynolds as co-commissioner. The United States already held all the Sac and Fox territory on the east bank of the Mississippi, and

Scott was instructed by Secretary of War Cass to demand a piece of their land running along the west bank as well. Cass's purpose was to cut the Sac and Fox off from immediate contact with white settlers. The fact that the majority of the tribe under Keokuk had always yielded peacefully to white demands, and that the antiwhite faction under Black Hawk had been largely exterminated, made no difference to Cass. The entire tribe must suffer.

The Winnebago and other tribes whose members had given any assistance to Black Hawk were also to be punished. If a large part of any tribe had taken part in the hostilities, all of that tribe's land east of the Mississippi was to be taken away. Where a smaller portion had been involved, the tribe was to lose the same percentage of land as the percentage of involved members. All individuals, of any tribe, who had taken part in the fighting were to be moved west of the Mississippi.

The peace councils were delayed by an outbreak of cholera toward the end of August. Negotiations with the Sac and Fox finally began on September 19, with Keokuk acting for the tribes. Traditionally only a civil chief should have been their spokesman on such an occasion. Keokuk was actually a war chief, being unqualified for the office of civil leader, a position which had to be inherited. But, at the beginning of the council, the American commissioners appointed him a civil chief, though they had no right to do so. Their purpose was to give him more status among the tribes. The commissioners preferred dealing with Keokuk, rather than with someone less friendly to the whites, and wanted to strengthen his position for that reason.

The treaty called for the surrender of a strip of land fifty miles wide along the west bank of the Mississippi, partly to compensate the United States for the "great expense of treasure" required to subdue the "formidable band" under "lawless and desperate leaders" and "partly to secure the future safety and tranquility" of the frontier. The strip ran from what is now the southern border of Iowa almost to the present northern boundary, with the exception of a small reservation of four hundred square miles within the strip. The United States gained six million acres which, within a few years, were valued at over seven million dollars. To avoid the misunderstandings of the treaty of 1804, the Indians were to be off these grounds by the following June. They were never to "reside, plant, fish, or hunt on any portion of the ceded country" after June 1, 1833.

The commissioners were not unaware of the enormous value of this war prize, for the third article of the treaty said: "In consideration of the great extent of the foregoing cession," the United States would pay the tribes twenty thousand dollars a year for the next thirty years. This would come to six hundred thousand dollars, a small fraction of what the land was worth. The United States also agreed to supply, every year for the same period of thirty years, forty kegs of tobacco and forty barrels of salt, and to set up a "Black and Gun Smith shop." In addition, the forty thousand dollars owed by the tribes to their traders, Farnham and Davenport, would be paid by the American government. And finally, as "a striking evidence of their mercy & liberality," the United States would immediately present the tribes, principally for the use of women and children who had lost their husbands and fathers in the war, with "thirty five beef cattle; twelve bushels of salt; thirty barrels of pork and fifty barrels of flour . . . and six thousand bushels of maize or Indian corn."

All the war prisoners, except for the leaders, were to be released in the custody of those Sac and Fox who had remained neutral during the hostilities. The Sioux would be "influenced" to release any Sac and Fox captives still held by them. The leaders—Black Hawk and his two sons, the

Prophet and his brother and two sons, Neapope, and four other chiefs—would be held indefinitely as hostages for the future good conduct of the tribes.

The treaty was signed on September 21, 1832. Nine Sacs, including Keokuk, and twenty-four Foxes signed for the Indians; Winfield Scott and John Reynolds, for the United States. On the day after the signing a great celebration was held, with an elaborate dinner, band music, and a dazzling display of fireworks, greatly admired by the Indians. In return Keokuk and his tribesmen put on a pantomime of a war expedition, followed by a war dance. The white audience applauded warmly. All those present, white and Indian, thoroughly enjoyed themselves.

But Black Hawk and his fellow war prisoners remained at Jefferson Barracks, miserable and uncertain of their future, if there was to be any future at all.

chapter fifteen

Great White Father

General Scott and Governor Reynolds suggested to Secretary Cass that the hostages be held for at least ten years. But Scott soon changed his mind and said it would be enough to hold only the principal leaders and let the rest go. Cass agreed, and ordered Atkinson to turn the released men over to Keokuk.

Before Atkinson had time to act, a delegation led by Keokuk appeared at St. Louis to ask that the prisoners be freed. They were met by William Clark, who was still the Superintendent of Indian Affairs for the region. He promised to help them, though he knew that the discharge of some of the prisoners had already been decided upon. By saying nothing of this decision, he was able to get, in return for his offer of help, Keokuk's promise to be responsible for the future good behavior of the released men.

Accompanied by Clark, Keokuk and his delegation went on to Jefferson Barracks. They sailed on the *Warrior,* the same boat that had taken part in the last tragic action at the Bad Axe. When they reached the barracks, the prisoners were brought out, and once again the two rival chiefs stood face to face.

It was now March 1833. Black Hawk had endured seven months of captivity and looked it. He did not care for the food at the barracks and had lost weight. He was still wearing a ball and chain. Most of all, his face showed his great depression over the failure of his resistance, the loss of his role as an active leader of the Sac, and the long, unaccustomed restraint.

Keokuk, on the other hand, had risen in status since the end of the war. He was the unopposed leader of the tribe, the respected spokesman for the Sac and Fox in their dealings with the white man. He had dressed carefully for the present occasion, in a colorful outfit which included a brightly printed cotton shirt, a green blanket, and a patterned kerchief on his head. Around his neck and wrists dangled shiny brass rings, and as a final touch, he wore a large medal presented to him by the United States government.

The chagrin produced by the appearance of a flourishing rival was, however, offset by the presence of more welcome visitors. Black Hawk's wife, Singing Bird, and his daughter had come along with the delegation. His deep affection for them had often been noticed by white observers, and he was overjoyed to see them again. Another welcome visitor was the tribe's white trader who had brought Black Hawk a gift of dried venison "that reminded me of the former pleasures of my own wigwam."

The prisoners cheered up greatly when they heard that the delegation had come to ask for their freedom. Six of them were disappointed, however, when they learned that though the rest were to be released in custody of Keokuk, they were to be sent to new prisons in the East. The six were Black Hawk and his eldest son—called Nasheaskuk, or Whirling Thunder in English—Neapope, the Prophet and his son, and a lesser Sac leader named Pamaho, or Fast-Swimming Fish. They were to be transferred to Fortress Monroe at Old Point Comfort, Virginia, with a stopover in Washington so that President Jackson could take a look at these obstinate resisters of his removal policy.

They left for Washington almost at once. In spite of the unhappy purpose of the journey, Black Hawk found it of immense interest and left a detailed record that might have been written by an avid tourist. The party went by steamboat up the Ohio, which Black Hawk found "the prettiest river (except our Mississippi) that I ever saw." The names of all the towns they passed were explained to him. "The first is called Louisville, and is a very pretty village. . . . The next is Cincinnati. . . . a large and beautiful village [which] seemed to be in a thriving condition."

They left the boat at Wheeling and transferred to a stagecoach. The Indians found this an uncomfortable means of travel, as it jounced through the mountains. Yet in spite of his discomfort, Black Hawk was greatly impressed by the Cumberland Road: "It is astonishing to see what labor and pains the white people have had to make this road. . . . " He was even more astonished to see the many homes and small villages along the way, since the land appeared so inhospitable and mountainous. He could not understand why white men wanted to live on hills.

His greatest amazement came when they arrived at another road, "much more wonderful than that through the mountains. They call it a *rail road!* I examined it carefully, but need not describe it, as the whites know all about it." Though he still preferred horseback to any other method of travel, he conceded that the whites "certainly deserve great praise for their industry."

If Black Hawk found these aspects of white civilization of great interest and curiosity, he was no less an object of interest and curiosity himself to the whites along his route. Crowds lined the riverbanks and streets wherever he appeared, eager to see the "savage Indian" who had dared to oppose the United States Army. In the safe and long-settled East, Indians had become objects of curiosity, not fear. Indeed many Easterners, safely settled upon land that had been taken from the Indians in an earlier generation, sympathized with the displaced natives of their own time. In all the towns through which they passed, wrote Black Hawk, "many called upon us, and treated us with kindness."

Black Hawk was moved by the consideration shown him in these long-settled areas and was pleased, too, that the inhabitants appeared content to remain in their mountainous regions instead of pushing on to Indian land. They contrasted favorably with the frontiersmen he had met around Saukenuk. In his experience with whites, "I have learned that one great principle of *their religion* is, 'to do unto others as you wish them to do unto you!' These people in the mountains seem to act upon this principle; but the settlers on our frontiers and on our lands, seem never to think of it, if we are to judge by their actions."

They reached Washington at last and were taken to the White House to meet "our Great Father, the President. He looks as if he had seen as many winters as I have, and seems to be a *great brave! . . .* I think he is a good man. . . .

His wigwam is well furnished with every thing good and pretty, and is very strongly built." As the two proud men faced each other, there appeared a certain resemblance between them. They were the same age; both had aquiline noses and dark eyes that glanced about fiercely. Black Hawk had a single scalp-lock rising above a high forehead while Jackson had a high stiff brush of gray hair, giving the same effect of length and severity to both faces.

But Andrew Jackson was the powerful and successful head of a nation whose size and strength had been made more apparent each day of the Indians' journey to Washington. Black Hawk was the defeated leader of a tiny band of helpless tribesmen, and the Great White Father intended to keep him defeated and powerless. He informed the dismayed captives that they were to be confined in Fortress Monroe until the United States Government was satisfied that the Indians intended to keep the peace, with each other as well as with their white neighbors.

Black Hawk and the Prophet expressed astonishment. They thought they had come to Washington to hold council with the Great Father as other chiefs, including Keokuk, had done. They were wrong, of course, and had indeed been told at the beginning that they were being transferred to another fort. Perhaps the good treatment on the trip East had made them feel more like visitors than prisoners. Black Hawk must have quickly reminded himself that he was indeed just a prisoner because without further objection, "I concluded it was best to obey our Great Father, and say nothing contrary to his wishes."

Whatever the intentions of Jackson and the Secretary of War, the Indians were treated almost as visiting celebrities. Before going on to Fortress Monroe, they spent a few days in Washington, sightseeing and receiving visitors. "During our stay . . . we were called upon by many of the people, who treated us well, particularly the squaws! We visited the great *council house* of the Americans—the place where they keep their *big guns*—and all the public buildings." They were presented with white men's clothing, which Black Hawk kept to the end of his life.

At Fortress Monroe the favored treatment continued: "The war chief met us, on our arrival, and shook hands, and appeared glad to see me. He treated us with great friendship, and talked to me frequently. Previous to our leaving this fort, he gave us a feast, and made us some presents. . . . I was sorry to leave him . . . because he had treated me like a brother, during all the time I remained with him."

During their stay the Indians were allowed to move around freely within the boundaries of the post. The officers' wives presented them with gifts, and there were frequent visitors from outside the fort. Washington Irving came to see them and found the warriors anything but fearsome. Far from looking like the terrors of the frontier, which the Illinois settlers had considered them, they were "a forlorn crew, emaciated and dejected—the redoubtable chieftain himself, a meagre old man upwards of seventy. He has, however," continued Irving, "a fine head, a Roman style of face, and a prepossessing countenance."

The "fine head" impressed many artists who came to sketch the Indians. George Catlin had done portraits of them at Jefferson Barracks, and at Fortress Monroe portraits were done by Charles Bird King, John Wesley Jarvis, and Samuel M. Brookes.

Thirty years later Jefferson Davis was to be imprisoned in Fortress Monroe. He was treated with a good deal less kindness and as an altogether different kind of celebrity. The defeated leader of the Confederacy was kept in ankle irons and displayed to mocking crowds. His sense of failure and humiliation must have been far greater than anything suffered by Black Hawk, no matter how dejected the chief felt within the restraining walls.

chapter sixteen

White Man's World

Black Hawk and the five other captives entered Fortress Monroe at the end of April. After a month Secretary Cass announced that these tired, defeated men were no longer a menace to the United States and should be sent home. General Atkinson and Superintendent Clark agreed. Atkinson thought the prisoners should be handed over to the custody of Keokuk. Clark approved of this, saying he was convinced that the Indians were now "fully impressed with the utter folly & hopelessness of contending against the arms of the UStates." Releasing the prisoners, he added, would earn the gratitude of the tribes and enhance Keokuk's position as a leader in whom the white government had confidence. Both

Clark and Atkinson also suggested that the Indians be returned to their homes by way of the large Eastern cities, so
that they might get a better idea of the size and strength of
the United States.

On May 30, Cass ordered the prisoners released. They
were to be taken through Baltimore, Philadelphia, New
York, and Boston. On June 4, the prisoners left Fortress
Monroe after a farewell party. Black Hawk made a speech
expressing his appreciation to the commander of the fort.
"We have buried the tomahawk," he said, "and the sound of
the rifle will hereafter only bring death to the deer and the
buffalo. . . . The memory of your friendship will remain
till the Great Spirit says it is time for Black Hawk to sing his
death-song."

Accompanied by Major John Garland, the Indians went
first to Norfolk, Virginia. A crowd gathered below the bal-
cony of their hotel room to see the celebrated warriors. The
Winnebago Prophet, discovering the pleasures of addressing
an attentive white audience, made the first of many similar
speeches. "We will go home with peaceable dispositions towards our white brethren," he said, "and make our conduct
hereafter, more satisfactory to them."

They were taken to see the navy yard at Gosport, where
they were greatly impressed by the *Delaware,* a seventy-four–
gun ship. The next day they went to Baltimore, staying at the
Fountain Inn on Light Street. "We were astonished to see so
large a village; but the war chief [Major Garland] told us
that we would soon see a *larger one.* This surprised us more."
They went sight-seeing and "saw much to admire."

It was just at this time that President Jackson began a trip
of his own through the Eastern cities. Either by coincidence
or bad planning, Black Hawk and Jackson came to several
of these cities at the same time. The dignified old Indian
chief drew almost as much attention as the head of the Amer-

ican nation. To Jackson's irritation, the crowds that greeted him in Baltimore, Philadelphia, and New York were hardly larger than those that came to see Black Hawk and his group. Black Hawk's eldest son, Whirling Thunder, was especially popular. He was a tall, handsome young man, whom one newspaper reporter described as "in nature and figure, a perfect Apollo." Other reporters called him Tommy Hawk, and several white, enthusiastic "pretty squaws" kissed him. He looked like the classic "noble savage," and the crowds were delighted with him.

In Baltimore, Black Hawk was taken to the theater. President Jackson was there for the same performance. "Our Great Father," wrote Black Hawk, ". . . seemed to be much liked by his white children, who flocked around him, (as they had done us,) to shake him by the hand." The next day Black Hawk was brought to see Jackson, who said, "You will see that our young men are as numerous as the leaves in the woods. What can you do against us?" By the end of his trip Black Hawk admitted the truth of these words.

The Indians next went to Philadelphia, arriving just after Jackson reached it. Again crowds of almost the same size turned out for both celebrities. Black Hawk was struck by the vast population and size of the city, "so much larger than the one we had left; but the war chief again told us, that we would soon see another much larger than this. I had no idea that the white people had such large villages, and so many people." He found them very agreeable, "very kind to us— showed us all their great public works, their ships and steam boats. . . . the place where they make money." This last was, of course, the mint, and Black Hawk was pleased with the newly minted coins presented to the Indians.

He also saw some military maneuvers in Philadelphia. "The chiefs and men were well dressed, and exhibited quite a warlike appearance," though he privately thought the Indi-

ans' own "system of military parade far better than that of
the whites."

On June 14, they reached New York City, the *big village*
whose great size he had been so astonished to hear about.
Here, too, Jackson's route coincided with that of the Indians,
who were amazed at the size of the crowds that came out to
greet them and the President. Black Hawk was now beginning to get some idea of the numbers and power of the people he had tried to oppose. Major Garland reported to the
Secretary of War that "It was with difficulty they could believe their own senses, when these populous cities and the
immense crowds of people . . . were placed before their
view; they had not formed even a distant conception of the
extent and population of the United States. . . ."

The crowd waiting to see the Indians was so large that
their carriage could not make its way through to the hotel
originally selected, and they had to go to the Exchange Hotel
on Broad Street instead. Black Hawk, who was rapidly becoming sophisticated about the white man's world, was
pleased with the "good rooms, good provisions, and every
thing necessary for our comfort." They were taken to several
theatrical performances and other "places of amusement.
. . . truly astonishing, yet very gratifying" and to public
buildings and gardens. At Castle Garden there were fireworks, "quite an agreeable entertainment—but to the
whites who witnessed it, less *magnificent* than the sight of
one of our large *prairies* would be when on fire."

As in the other cities, leading residents came to see the Indians in their hotel suite. Many brought gifts, including a
pair of topaz earrings for Singing Bird. In expressing his
thanks, Black Hawk said, "Brother, we like your talk. We will
be friends. We like the white people. They are very kind to
us. We will not forget it. . . ." Everyone, he wrote later,
"treated us with friendship, and many with great liberality,"

especially the white squaws, who "were very kind, very good and very pretty—for *pale faces!*"

The most awesome sight in New York was a balloon ascension, which took place just as the boat bringing them to the city was pulling up at the wharf: "We had seen many wonderful sights . . . large villages, the great *national road* over the mountains, the *rail-roads,* steam carriages, ships, steam boats, and many other things; but we were now about to witness a sight more surprising than any of these. We were told that a man was going up into the air in a balloon! We watched with anxiety to see if it could be true; and to our utter astonishment, saw him ascend in the air until the eye could no longer perceive him." When the balloon began to descend, the crowds turned their attention to Black Hawk, who was preparing to disembark. He raised his hat to them and said, "How do you do? How do you do all? The Great Spirit knows that I love you, and that my heart is with you." A newspaper reporter asked him what he thought of the balloon ascension. Black Hawk replied: "That man is brave— don't think he will ever get back."

If the Indians had required any further proof of the power and bravery of the whites, the balloon ascension was the final touch. Taking Black Hawk home by way of the great Eastern cities had been a shrewd procedure. As he saw "village" after "village," each larger than the one before, each with larger crowds of people, he realized more fully the hopelessness of making war upon the whites. He saw that in addition to their endless numbers of young men—"as numerous as the leaves in the woods," Jackson had said—the Americans had vast supplies of war materials and many ingenious methods of transporting this great wealth of men and supplies. How could the Indians hope to succeed against cannon and steamships? At the end of his trip Black Hawk told a Seneca chief, "Brother, we have seen how great a people the whites are. They are very rich and very strong—it is folly for us to fight them."

Perhaps if Black Hawk had been taken to the East before all the trouble began, to see for himself just what he would be up against in defying white demands, the war might never have taken place. He might have followed the advice of Keokuk and retreated quietly, if unhappily, to the west bank of the Mississippi. As time went on, government authorities came to believe that a personal view of white power was the strongest deterrent to Indian resistance. Thousands of native leaders were brought to Washington on state visits, to see with their own eyes the nation's power and wealth, and to be convinced of the hopelessness of trying to fight the white man. The expense of such Indian junkets was only a trifle compared to what it cost to subdue the Indians by military means. And when such entertainments resulted in land acquisitions, as they so often did, the relatively small expense was considered infinitely worthwhile.

The next stop was supposed to be Boston, but by this time Black Hawk was tired. He had seen enough and was worn out by the many public appearances, the speeches, the crowds. The unaccustomed noise had left "a buzzing in my ears." He longed to return to his own people and his own way of living. Major Garland was willing to cut the trip short, and probably just as happy to avoid competing again with President Jackson who was also heading toward Boston. Instead Major Garland took his Indians on a steamer up the Hudson River to Albany where again large crowds waited along the shore.

Part of the journey home was made by Great Lakes steamer, with a visit to Detroit on the way. At Green Bay, Wisconsin, they left the Lakes, went up the Fox River, then down the Wisconsin River to the Mississippi. At Prairie du Chien the Prophet and his son left the party to join their own tribe farther north. Black Hawk and the others continued down the Mississippi to Fort Armstrong on Rock Island.

Black Hawk was back in his own country. But nothing would ever be the same again.

part three

SURVIVAL

chapter one

Retired Warrior

Of all the changes in Black Hawk's life, perhaps the hardest to accept was his subordination to Keokuk. When the returning Indians arrived at Rock Island, a council was called with the Sac and Fox leaders. Major Garland announced that the object of the council was to deliver Black Hawk up to Keokuk. He read a message from President Jackson stating that Keokuk was recognized as the head of the Sac nation and directing Black Hawk "to follow Keokuk's advice, and be governed by his counsel in all things." The appalled Black Hawk leaped to his feet at this, and cried out that no one was going to tell him what to do. He was "mortified," his "feelings of pride and honor insulted." Unable to say more because of his intense agitation, he sat down.

Keokuk now stepped in and, in his characteristic way, calmed Black Hawk and assured the white authorities present that there would be no further trouble. Black Hawk himself, realizing that he was no longer in any position to take defiant postures, apologized for his outburst. "I am sorry that I was so hasty in reply . . . because I said that which I did not intend." He added that he hoped his words would not be repeated to the President for, as Garland reported it, he had given Jackson "his word that he would remain at peace and he intended to do it."

Black Hawk kept his word. With the rest of the Sac and Fox, now numbering about six thousand for the combined tribes, he settled near the Iowa River. He and his wife, their two sons and pretty daughter, lived in a lodge of peeled bark. Joseph Street, the tribes' Indian Bureau agent, gave him a cow. A visitor to his lodge found it "a specimen of neatness and good order." At the tribal councils he remained in the background or out of things altogether. The old warrior had really retired at last.

Like many of the displaced tribes, the Sac and Fox found it difficult to adjust to their new lives. Hunting, which had been one of the foundations of their existence, grew poorer each year as the game diminished and the number of hunters increased. As more Indians were forced into the region west of the Mississippi, and as more white hunters crossed into the territory, the competition for buffalo, deer, beaver, otter, muskrat, and raccoon grew sharper. The animals were not only being killed off more rapidly by the competing hunters, but as the area grew more populated, whatever game was left drew back to less inhabited regions. When the Indians pursued the game to these remoter grounds, they ran into hostile tribes. There were more encounters between the Sac and Fox and the Sioux, and the old animosity flared up in violent intertribal warfare.

The Plains Indians, the original inhabitants of the trans-Mississippi region at the time of removal, did not welcome the newly arriving eastern Indians who had been compelled to leave their old homes east of the river. The western Indians regarded the newcomers as intruders who were seriously disturbing their way of life. The addition of a hundred thousand eastern Indians, most of them hunters, threatened to destroy the principal source of food. The Plains Indians also claimed that much of the land allotted to the newcomers by the United States was the rightful property of Plains tribes and bitterly contested the new arrangements.

The eastern tribes, in their turn, looked down upon the Plains Indians as barbarians, or "wild tribes." As more easterners kept crowding into the Plains area, the antagonism between the two groups increased. When the immigrant Indians went out to hunt the Plains buffalo, bands of Plains warriors raided the property of the immigrants. The United States had promised to protect the displaced eastern Indians, but like many government promises, this one was inadequately kept. Much of the time the newcomers were forced to defend themselves, and open conflict was common. In an attempt to keep peace among the tribes, the government established army posts along the western frontier. But the posts were undermanned, and the intervals of peace were filled with uncertainty. The "Indian problem" was still far from being solved, despite the glowing promises of Jackson's removal policy.

The Plains Indians might have been considered primitive by the more sophisticated eastern Indians, but they could outride and outhunt the easterners in the competition for the dwindling game. Some of the hunters among the new arrivals, including many Sac and Fox, became depressed by the scarcity of game and the obstacles to getting it. Hunting and trapping were no longer profitable. Instead of piling up skins for trading purposes, the hunters found themselves piling up debts to the traders for the traps and other supplies needed in advance for the annual hunts. They began to cut down on their hunting, but found little to replace it.

The United States Indian Bureau had hoped to transform the warriors into farmers, but among the northern Indians agriculture had always been a woman's occupation, and the braves were not ready to take it over. The Sac women continued to cultivate small patches of corn, melons, beans, and squash on soil less fertile than around Saukenuk while the men did nothing. They preferred to scrape along on the annuities received for the sale of their land and to hang around the white settlements during the winter seasons which had formerly been spent in hunting.

The results were disquieting. Deprived of the strong traditional framework of their lives, the satisfying round of hunting, farming, ceremonials, and feasts as the seasons changed, the Indians sank into a demoralizing apathy. With the old rhythm of life destroyed, the principal escape from the new emptiness was through alcohol. Unscrupulous white traders knew that the Indians, with no knowledge of real market values, would exchange anything for liquor. Valuable horses, guns, and furs were given for small quantities of whisky, and the whisky jug often contained as much water as spirits. Intoxication rose sharply among the Indians, and with it came brawling and disorder. Sac and Fox chiefs, who had always frowned on the use of liquor and had opposed the sale of it to their warriors, now drank along with the rest, until one government report described the tribal leaders themselves as "inveterate sots."

And the land cessions continued. Although the Mississippi River was supposed to be the great dividing line between Indians and whites, the whites kept crossing it. Between 1830 and 1850 the Great Lakes area filled up with farmers coming from New England and the Middle Atlantic States as factories replaced farmland in those regions. Pushing beyond the Mississippi, the displaced farmers discovered the grass-covered prairies of Iowa. They urged the Federal Government to open the area to settlement. The treaty concluding the Black Hawk War was the first step. Less than a year after the treaty was signed and even before Black Hawk returned home, the Iowa holdings of the Sac and Fox conceded by this treaty were opened to white farmers.

The rush of settlers was quickened by enticing descriptions of the new land. An enthusiastic reporter for a Buffalo newspaper wrote: "Taking into consideration the soil, the timber, the water and the climate, Iowa territory may be considered the best part of the Mississippi Valley. The Indians so considered it, as appears from the name which they gave it. For it is said that the Sac and Fox Indians, on beholding the exceeding beauties of this region, held up their hands, and exclaimed in an ecstasy of delight and amazement, 'Iowa,' which in the Fox language means, 'this is the land.' "

By 1836 ten thousand whites had settled there, and more were coming. As new communities were established, the usual friction between the settlers and Indians broke out. Keokuk, realizing that he could not prevent "the great fog of white people which is rolling toward the setting sun," offered to sell the reservation which the tribe had retained on the Iowa River. The reservation was too close to the encroaching whites and he wanted to move further away from "the great fog." A more compelling reason might have been the need for money to pay off the tribes' debts, which mounted seriously as the hunting declined.

The reservation, known as the Keokuk Reserve, consisted of four hundred square miles. Colonel Henry Dodge, who had fought against Black Hawk, acted for the government in the negotiations. He urged Keokuk to sell all of the tribal lands in Iowa and move his people south of the Missouri River. Keokuk refused, and kept to his original proposal. He asked $1.25 an acre for 256,000 acres. Dodge countered with 75 cents, and 75 cents was what the tribes finally got. Since the steadily arriving settlers would be glad to pay three dollars an acre, the United States had made another profitable land deal.

The treaty was signed in September 1836. George Catlin, the painter, was at the negotiations and was struck by the unhappy appearance of Black Hawk: "The poor dethroned monarch, old Black Hawk, was present, and looked an object of pity. With an old frock coat and brown hat on, and a cane in his hand, he stood the whole time outside of the group, and in dumb and dismal silence. . . ."

In sharp contrast, Keokuk was in his glory. He wore white buckskins and, draped around his right arm, a snakeskin decorated with little bells that jingled as he made oratorical points. His horse had a silver saddle. Both whites and Indians accepted him as the leader and chief spokesman for his people.

Keokuk took full advantage of his position. He had insisted that tribal annuities be paid not to individual members but to the chiefs, explaining that he would see to the distribution of the money. This meant that he could hold back payment from anyone who displeased him or refused to accept his authority. His vanity and ambitiousness became more evident as the American authorities paid more attention to him. Finding Keokuk easy to deal with, they presented him with many gifts and invited him to councils and ceremonies at which he was treated with great respect. Keokuk enjoyed this kind of flattery. Yet he never gave way to white demands just to feed his own ego or fatten his own pocket. He defended the rights of the combined tribes firmly and eloquently against any demands that he considered unjust. But he was never unrealistic, as Black Hawk had been. He accepted the inevitable gracefully, a position that the whites found highly convenient and for which they openly showed their appreciation.

The whites may have admired Keokuk, but an increasing number of Sac and Fox grew disenchanted with him. They resented his use of annuity money to enforce his power. They felt that too much of it found its way to his personal friends. The Fox, especially, disliked his methods of handling tribal money. Dissidents among both tribes were irked by the expensive way in which Keokuk lived, with his fine horses and good brandy, after the manner of the whites. He traveled a great deal, always in high style, dressed in fine clothes and surrounded by an impressive retinue of followers.

The opposition to Keokuk became stronger after a second land cession in 1837, just a year after the first. This became known as the Second Black Hawk Purchase and consisted of 1,250,000 acres just west of the land lost in 1832. In addition to the usual payment of tribal debts and annuities, the United States presented the tribal delegation sent to negotiate the treaty with $4500 in gifts and a guided all-expense tour of the large Eastern cities. Keokuk was, of course, the leader of the group. Besides the gifts and free excursion, he received still another benefit: while the rest of the tribesmen had to be off the ceded land within eight months, Keokuk's own village was permitted to remain for two years.

The resentment aroused by all of this deepened the splits that had already appeared. The Fox tribe began to think of itself as a separate group once more, while pro- and anti-Keokuk factions developed among the Sac. The anti-Keokuk faction almost succeeded in replacing him with a chief named Hardfish, who had a hereditary right to the chieftainship which Keokuk lacked, but white support helped Keokuk retain his position.

Black Hawk, though no longer active in the increasingly acrimonious tribal politics, remained opposed to Keokuk. At the Independence Day celebration in Fort Madison in 1838, where Black Hawk was a guest of honor, he said: "I was once a great warrior. I am now poor. Keokuk has been the cause of my present situation."

This was, perhaps, not altogether fair. It is highly doubtful that Black Hawk could have done much better against the United States Army even with the full cooperation of Keokuk. But it was certainly true that with the rise of his rival as the most important man in the tribe, at least in the eyes of the whites, Black Hawk's position became correspondingly lower. And it was always Keokuk he blamed, never the whites. "I feel grateful to the whites for the kind manner they treated me and my party, whilst travelling among them— and from my heart I assure them, that the white man will always be welcome . . . as a brother. The tomahawk is buried forever! We will forget what has past—and may the watchword between the Americans and Sacs and Foxes, ever be—'*Friendship!*' "

chapter two

The Last Word

In 1838, at the age of seventy-one, Black Hawk moved for the last time. He and his family left their lodge on the Iowa River and went to a new spot on the Des Moines River, near the present town of Iowaville. Soon afterward, on October 3 of the same year, he died. Following the traditional custom of the Sac, his body was placed in a sitting position in a small log structure. He was dressed in a military uniform that President Jackson had given to him in Washington back in 1832. A military hat with feathers was put on his head. At his left was placed a sword; at his right were two canes, one a gift from Henry Clay, the other from a British army officer. Around his neck hung three medals, suspended from ribbons. One had been given to him by Jackson, another by John Quincy Adams, the third by the city of Boston.

Sods of bluegrass were placed over the wooden structure, making a mound about four feet high. At the head of the mound a twenty-foot flagstaff was placed, flying a silk American flag, and nearby stood a post carved with his feats of bravery. A high picket fence enclosed the grave.

Less than a year later the grave was robbed by a white man, Dr. James Turner, who removed the skeleton, intending to put it on exhibition. Black Hawk's sons protested angrily to the governor of Iowa Territory. Governor Lucas had the bones brought to Burlington, the territorial capital, and sent word to Black Hawk's sons to call for them. When the sons came to the courthouse and discovered that their father's bones were being stored in a "good, dry place," they decided to leave them there, feeling it was as safe a burial place as any. About a year or two later, the bones were transferred to the museum of the Burlington Geological and Historical Society, where they remained until 1855 when a great fire destroyed the building and its contents.

Black Hawk's bones were lost, but there were other, more enduring monuments to his memory. In 1911, Lorado Taft, the famous Illinois sculptor, created a fifty-foot concrete statue of Black Hawk near Oregon, Illinois, on a high bluff overlooking the old chief's beloved Rock River. Taft chose his subject because he felt that Black Hawk was a representative Indian patriot. At the unveiling of the statue, one of the speakers described the figure as "not sullen, not resentful, not despondent, not surrendering, but simple, unflinching, erect; with the pathos of his past in his face, the tragedy of the future in his eyes; but with the dauntless courage of a man in his whole figure and attitude."

Near Rock Island there is the two-hundred—acre Black

Hawk State Park, with a museum containing a famous collection of Indian relics. Though the park was not officially created until 1927, it is often called the oldest park in the Midwest, since it lies on the exact spot used by the Sac and Fox for their feasts and games. Another "Black Hawk Monument" stands in Stillman's Valley. South of Rockford, the Black Hawk Indian Trail leads hikers and motorists right through the Rock River country. And his name is also being kept alive by one of professional hockey's most famous teams, the Chicago Black Hawks.

Perhaps the best memorial of all, the one that would have pleased the old chief best, is the fact that it is Black Hawk, not Keokuk, who is regarded as the great hero of the Sac. Black Hawk defended a hopeless cause while Keokuk, through his skillful negotiations and diplomatic relations with the whites, managed to salvage land and rights that the recalcitrant war chief might have lost altogether. Nevertheless, Black Hawk remains the brave who resisted white pressure, the stubborn patriot who fought for ancestral lands and traditions, while Keokuk is considered the compromiser, the yielder.

chapter three

As Long As Grass

Grows

After the Black Hawk War, the Sac and Fox had the same unhappy experiences suffered by most of the tribes that gave up their lands and moved west. Whether they went voluntarily, as advised by men like Keokuk, or were driven out by force, like Black Hawk, in the long run the results were the same.

In announcing the removal policy, Jackson had promised that if the Indians would move beyond the Mississippi, they could live there happily ever after, undisturbed by the white man and uncorrupted by contact with his civilization. "Their white brethren will not trouble them, they [the whites] will have no claim to the land." The Indians could remain securely in their new homes, "they and all their children, as long as grass grows or waters run, in peace and plenty." But only thirteen years after the Sac and Fox had moved beyond the Mississippi to Iowa, the press of white settlement forced them to move again.

The same thing happened to tribe after tribe, though the grass was still growing and the water still running. In fact, it was largely because of the grass and water that the Indians had to move, to make way for the land-hungry whites. It was only in those areas short of grass and water, on land considered unfit for white farming or undesirable for white life, as in the arid Southwest where tribes like the Hopi and Havasupi lived, that the Indians were permitted to remain undisturbed.

By 1840, there were forty-three thousand whites living in Iowa, and the demand for more land was renewed. In 1842, yielding to the double pressures of government urging and mounting debts, the Sac and Fox reluctantly sold the rest of their Iowa holdings, about ten million acres of prime land.

They were permitted to remain until 1845, when they were moved south of the Missouri to the headwaters of the Osage River in Kansas. Here they crowded into a reservation already occupied by the Ottawa, Chippewa, and Kansas tribes. The soil was poor, too sandy for the type of farming done by the Sac and Fox. Too little rainfall, too many grasshoppers, reduced the crops still more, and the Indians often went hungry.

Hunting was bad, with most of the small game vanished and the buffalo plains cut off by hostile tribes. Cholera, measles, and smallpox reduced still further the steadily declining numbers of the Sac and Fox. Worst of all was the fading away of hope.

The United States offered to prepare the Indians for a better future through education, but even the progressive Keokuk rejected any attempt to introduce the white man's schoolhouse. The Indians' experience with brutal frontiersmen, cheating traders, and corrupt government agents had left them with little respect for white culture. Nor had the behavior of frontier settlers and authorities given them a high opinion of Christian ethics and morality. Education, in the white man's sense, held no attractions for them.

Under these conditions, drunkenness increased, and so did the division into quarreling factions. Some tribesmen broke away altogether. About a hundred, mostly Foxes, returned to Iowa where, surprisingly, they were accepted by the white settlers. The presence of only a few Indians did not constitute a menace, and they were useful as a source of cheap farm labor. They also provided a good market for local whisky dealers. From time to time others quarreled with the main group and left to join those in Iowa.

Those who remained in Kansas were soon to be disturbed

Land ceded by the Sac and Fox to the United States

again by the continued pressure of the expanding nation. This time the need for new railroad routes was added to the old reasons for moving the Indians. But the old techniques were still used. Squatters trespassed on Indian lands, destroying Indian garden patches, stealing Indian ponies, and generally causing trouble between the races.

Once again the Indians were subjected to an official removal policy. This time a number of tribes were resettled in the Indian Territory, the present state of Oklahoma. To make room for them, tribes already in the area had to be shunted around. So many Indians were transplanted from one spot to another that one chief asked, "Why does not the Great Father put his red children on wheels, so he can move them as he will?"

The Sac and Fox were shifted to Oklahoma after twenty-three years in Kansas. This was their third move to the "permanent home of the tribe FOREVER," promised by the American government. Here, too, the land was poor, the rainfall too scanty for productive farming, and the hunting worse than ever. There was nothing for the braves to do; they passed the time in gambling, horse racing, visiting with friends. The government tried to interest them in agriculture, but there were too many obstacles. Besides the poor quality of the land, which would discourage even experienced farmers, the Indians had none of the necessary equipment. They lacked the basic tools and animals for successful agriculture, and had neither money nor credit with which to buy them. Above all, how could warriors who still talked about the great, adventurous days of Sac and Fox military glory under such leaders as Black Hawk settle down to routine farming? How could they turn to any kind of dull, tedious labor while they still remembered the exhilaration of the hunt, the wonderfully free existence among the beautiful woods and streams of their original home?

The aim of the government was to "acculturate" the Indians: to get rid of the tribal form of life and turn the Indian into a white man, living and working as an individual. Even sympathetic friends of the Indian overlooked the fact that an Indian might not want to be assimilated into white society—even if that society would have accepted him, which it often refused to do. The Indian preferred his tribal organization and would have felt lost without it. There were many aspects of white civilization the Indian was willing and often glad to adopt: machines and manufactured goods of all kinds, from tools to factory-made clothing. But when it came to social and religious forms, he wanted to keep his own.

The government felt that if the Indian could be introduced to the concept of private property, it might hasten his assimilation into the white world. In 1887, therefore, the Dawes Act was passed, authorizing the President, at his discretion, to divide the lands of a tribe into individual allotments. The head of a family would receive 160 acres; women, children, and unmarried men would receive smaller amounts. Any tribal land remaining after such division would be sold by the government, with the proceeds to go to the tribesmen.

The sale of surplus reservation land to white settlers resulted in a series of famous land rushes. Over a hundred thousand impatient land seekers and speculators took part in a dramatic rush to claim the first homesteads when these were thrown open to the public at noon on April 22, 1889. At the end of the day, 1,920,000 acres of the land that had been given to the Indians forever had been taken over by whites. Ten thousand settlers put up tents that first night in the suddenly created Oklahoma City. Similar rushes took place every time a new section of reservation land was put on the open market.

In 1891 the allotment policy reached the Sac and Fox,

over the opposition of the majority of the tribesmen. Most tribes were opposed to allotment, but there was no way for them to stop it. Keokuk's grandson went with a delegation to Washington to protest the division of tribal lands, but the government went ahead anyway.

The white agent for the Sac and Fox hoped that the Indians would learn the "arts and methods of agriculture" from their new white neighbors. But the same obstacles—poor land, lack of equipment, capital, and farm animals, and lack of agricultural training and interest—operated on the individual holdings as on the reservation. The individual holdings were under government trusteeship for twenty-five years, which meant that Indians could not get mortgages or loans as white farmers could. The few Indians who did manage to establish farms found themselves heavily taxed. Any improvements, such as wells and plowed land, and all articles of personal property were taxed at a high rate. The effect was to discourage improvements. Some Indian farmers found themselves taxed out of existence; others did not even try to become farmers in the face of such odds.

Many Indians simply leased their land to white farmers, who often managed to defraud their native landlords in some way. Others worked as hired hands for their white neighbors. When the twenty-five-year trust period expired, many sold their holdings to whites for the usual rock-bottom prices. Then, with no experience in handling or investing such sums, they dribbled away the purchase price and were left with neither land nor money. In 1912 oil was discovered on Indian land, but by the time the income from oil leases was divided among the tribes, it amounted to about forty dollars a year for each member.

Even before the breakup of tribal lands, the Sac and Fox tribal organization had begun to disintegrate, and allotment hastened the process. Several years after allotment, the Secretary of the Interior abolished the traditional tribal council. It was replaced by a three-man business committee which was given so little power that it eventually disappeared.

As a result of the allotment act, by 1932 some ninety million acres had been transferred to white ownership. The Indians had not been assimilated and were worse off than ever. Those who remained on the reservations were still regarded as wards of the government. They were not permitted to manage their own affairs or to have a voice in decisions affecting their own lives. Given no responsibility or motivation, it was easy for them to lose their spirit and initiative and to lapse into a state of patient, apathetic endurance. Those who left the reservations had little preparation for living and working in the white world and, all too often, sank to the bottom level of existence in that world.

The lack of preparation was due mainly to the poor state of Indian education. Reservation schools were run by white administrators who had little understanding of the real needs of Indian children. Indian adults were not consulted, nor were they given any significant role in running the schools. Teachers were often the wives or relatives, scarcely educated themselves, of local Indian Bureau agents.

Subjects were selected with no consideration of what was really desirable for Indian children. There was a strong emphasis on vocational or manual labor courses, which the Indians found too limited or distasteful. Girls, for example, were trained in domestic work with an eye to their becoming servants, an occupation despised by Indians. Boys were trained to do routine farm work, as though no other career beside farming were possible for Indian boys. The children were unused to the strict discipline, so different from the easy-going atmosphere of tribal life. At times the schools were run by one of the Christian religious denominations, which the Indians resented. It is not surprising that even when schools were made available on the reservations, the tribesmen were reluctant to send their children to them, or if the children did attend, they quickly became discouraged and dropped out.

Worst of all was the system of Indian boarding schools that began in the 1870s. Children were sent off the reservation, away from their homes, to schools where the primary aim seemed to be to break all ties with Indian life. The children, many of them forcibly taken from their families, were made to feel that everything Indian was inferior. The goal was to "civilize" them; in the process they were deprived of their unique heritage as Indians. They were forbidden to speak their own tribal language or wear tribal dress and hair styles. Their customs and religious ceremonies were ridiculed. In one school, the mouths of the children were washed out with soap if they "spoke Indian."

Accustomed to warm relationships with adults, the boarding-school children were disheartened by the impersonal treatment of the professional staff. There were cases of lonely, depressed children committing suicide. To add to the general unhappiness, the children were frequently half starved, with less than seven cents a day spent on each pupil for food. Even as late as 1968, Senator Robert Kennedy was shocked to learn that the Bureau of Indian Affairs was spending only twenty-two cents a meal. The students were constantly urged not to return to their reservations. Going "back to the blanket" was considered by their white teachers as a sign of personal failure.

The young Indians who managed to get through such schools and those who went on to college found life difficult after graduation. They could no longer feel at home in their own world, nor could they fit easily into white society. Among the whites they often felt alien and inferior. In some areas there were social or economic barriers. They were faced with the problem, common to minorities and to the children of immigrants, of being suspended between two cultures, unable to become totally absorbed in either one or to participate successfully in both. No attempt had been made to educate the Indian child as both an Indian and an American, understanding and appreciating both cultures, and prepared to live in either one or to combine the two. Today the eighty-one Indian boarding schools currently in existence are still being accused of turning out "no-culture people," unable to identify with either their Indian heritage or the "hostile white world."

The problem was more difficult for the young Indian than for the child of European immigrants, since the gap between the old and the new culture was much greater for the Indian. Even when he managed to bridge the gap, he found it hard to shake off his "Indianness." The forms and values of Indian tribal life were so deeply a part of his nature that he could not easily abandon them, especially if he found little to take their place. And, like the black American, the Indian had to face the added handicap of racial intolerance.

There were, of course, some young Indians who had good educational experiences, particularly if they were lucky enough to have skills admired by both cultures. Jim Thorpe, the great athlete who led the famous football team at the Carlisle Indian School, was one of these. Wa-tho-huck—his Indian name, meaning Bright Path—was a Sac and Fox, the grandson of Black Hawk's daughter. His superior ability in track, field, and baseball, as well as football, and his Olympic championships in the pentathlon and decathlon, won him acceptance in both worlds. There is also Maria Tallchief, a member of the Osage tribe, who became one of America's foremost ballet dancers. Her outstanding talents were recognized not only by the white world but by her own people, who presented her with the 1967 Indian Achievement Award.

Most of the Sac and Fox, however, objected to the kind of education provided for them. Eventually some children began attending the regular public schools. This was an advance over the old Indian agency or boarding schools, but the Indians still had nothing to say about the kind of education their children were getting, and it continued to be inadequate.

In the 1930s, as part of Franklin Delano Roosevelt's New Deal, the government dramatically reversed its Indian policy. The goal was no longer to de-Indianize the Indian, but to help him develop his own resources. The new Commissioner of Indian Affairs appointed by President Roosevelt was John Collier, a social scientist with an unusually sympathetic understanding of Indian life and problems. With the energetic backing of the new Secretary of the Interior, Harold Ickes, Collier completely remodeled the Indian Bureau. Allotment was abolished, tribal lands were reassembled when possible, and money was made available to buy new land. Financial aid and credit were provided for agricultural and industrial projects. Educational and medical facilities were established. Tribal organization and activities were, for the first time, encouraged. The ceremonials of Indian religions were no longer banned as they had been in earlier periods. Indian languages were no longer forbidden in the schools: some elementary textbooks were printed in Sioux and Navajo, and Indian teachers who could speak to the children in their own tongue were appointed.

Most of these reforms were embodied in the Indian Reorganization Act of 1934. Though many of its measures were poorly carried out or hampered by Congress's failure to appropriate enough money, it was, at least, the first constructive attempt to look at the situation from the Indian's point of view. Roosevelt and Collier believed that the American doctrine of personal and political liberty implied the right of the Indian to maintain his own tribal organization and to live according to his own beliefs and customs.

Many tribes took advantage of the financial opportunities now opened to them, but the Sac and Fox had lost the will to operate once more as a united tribe. They did reorganize their tribal government, with a chief and council, and adopt a new constitution, but it was little more than a formality. Most of the Sac and Fox drifted into the white world, with varying degrees of success. Yet there were still many who retained a deep tribal sentiment and who cherished the story of Black Hawk and his courageous attempt to resist white power.

In the years following the Indian Reorganization Act, the Federal government showed a tendency to return to its original policy of ending tribalism and pushing the Indian into the current of white life as quickly as possible. This was to be done whether the Indian wanted to join that current or not, whether he was ready or not. At the same time, government authorities were very slow in turning over to the Indians the responsibility of managing their own tribal and reservation affairs. Yet such responsibility would provide the best training for carrying out the government's own goal of getting the Indian to function in the white world.

One of the greatest barriers remains the failure to accept the Indian for what he is, whether he chooses to be part of a tribal culture with its own way of life or a voluntary participant in the majority society of the nation. The centuries of misunderstanding and mistreatment have left the Indians very suspicious of what might happen to them in that society. The anthropologist D'Arcy McNickle, himself a member of the Confederated Salish and Kootenai tribes, wrote that the

Indians "have a deep-seated conviction, rational or not, that once they cut loose from the past, abandon tribal ties, and commit themselves to urban-industrial existence, they will become a faceless people in an alien world. And that, in their instinctual thinking, would make their poverty unbearable. So long as they cling to a name, they have a destiny."

Since the Indian has long been thought of as "the vanishing American," it might come as a surprise to learn that he still has a destiny. Far from vanishing, the American Indian today retains a strong sense of himself, his values, his tribal relationships. His numbers are increasing. Until the beginning of the twentieth century, war, disease, starvation, and general hopelessness had caused the Indian population to drop steadily, until it seemed as though the original American would indeed vanish. But shortly after the start of the century, there was a sudden upturn. Since then the Indian population has doubled, and is rising far more rapidly than that of the rest of the country. The Navajos alone increased from twelve thousand in 1868 to almost a hundred thousand in 1968.

The Indian is also taking stronger measures today to protect and further his destiny. He is doing it, not as Black Hawk did by opposing military power with physical resistance, but by using modern methods of organized action. The Indians have begun at last to take Tecumseh's advice to join together for the common Indian good, to think of themselves not just as Sioux or Shawnee or Sac or Fox, but as Indians. National organizations, drawing membership from tribes all over the country, have been created to speak and act for all Indians. These organizations have been demanding that Indian rights and needs be respected, that Indian culture be respected and made part of their children's education. Such respect, together with a full voice in all decisions affecting him and a full share in carrying out these decisions, is long overdue the American Indian.

chapter four

Happy Buffalo and
Hungry Wolf

In 1833, after his return from the East, Black Hawk dictated his autobiography to Antoine LeClaire, the respected interpreter for the Indians of the region. John B. Patterson, a young editor and regimental printer to a militia company during the Black Hawk War, helped prepare the document for publication. A dominant theme of the book is Black Hawk's intense love for his own land and his anguish at being forced to leave it. The white man, he says, does not understand the special kinship that an Indian feels for his home. "It was here, that I was born—and here lie the bones of many friends and relations. For this spot I felt a sacred reverence, and never could consent to leave it, without being forced therefrom." But he was forced, with a catastrophic suddenness that he found hard to accept: "If another prophet had come to our village in those days, and told us what has since taken place, none of our people would have believed him. What! to be driven from our village and hunting grounds, and not even permitted to visit the graves of our forefathers, our relations, and friends? . . . How different is our situation now, from what it was in those days! Then we were as happy as the buffalo on the plains—but now, we are as miserable as the hungry, howling wolf in the prairie! . . . Bitter reflection crowds upon my mind, and must find utterance."

He asks over and over again: "Why did the Great Spirit ever send the whites . . . to drive us from our homes, and introduce among us poisonous liquors, disease and death? They should have remained on the island where the Great Spirit first placed them."

But the whites did come: it was inevitable that sooner or later they would find their way across the Atlantic. It was also inevitable that, with their advanced military and industrial techniques, they would take control of the continent away from the Indians. The Indians themselves had engaged in this kind of displacement process, with strong tribes forcing weaker ones to move. The powerful Iroquois tribes, for example, forced the Chippewa, Ottawa, and Potawatomi out of the East. These displaced tribes went to the Great Lakes region, forcing, in their turn, the Sac, Fox, Kickapoo, and Mascoutens to move south, pushing out the members of the Illinois confederation and the Miami.

When the Indians displaced each other, however, they did not destroy a way of life; they did not attempt to wipe out an entire culture. It was more of a jockeying back and forth, or a gradual pressure toward new areas enough like the old so that the fundamental patterns of living remained undamaged and generally unchanged.

The white invasion was as different in nature as it was in size. Here an overwhelming force swept down upon a relatively defenseless minority and drove it ruthlessly out of the way, destroying culture patterns, religions, and human dignity as well as lives in the process.

Looking at American history through Indian eyes, it would be easy to put it all down as a simple, though monstrous, case of injustice committed by a strong group upon a weaker one. But it is not that simple, and a completely just solution would have been far from easy, if not impossible. Even without the many crimes of the whites—the double-dealing, the broken treaties, the racial prejudice, the outright cruelties, the blind dogmatism of those who intended no physical harm but tried, often in the name of religion, to destroy the Indians' way of life or demean their dignity as a people—even without these, there would still have remained infinite complexities and difficulties.

The whites were not all villains, and the Indians were not all noble savages. There were blunders, atrocities, betrayals, and a ruinous lack of good judgment on both sides. Both sides killed and tortured innocent people with a variety of horrible methods. If there were corrupt values and sharp practices and hypocritical pietism among the whites, there were superstitions, ignorance, and dangerously primitive customs among many of the Indian tribes.

The question is not a simple matter of who was right or wrong, but of what happens—what can happen?—when a group barely emerging from the stone age, however excellent they may be in themselves, runs head on into another group thousands of years ahead in technical development, immensely larger in sheer numbers, and energetically bursting out of old boundaries? The whites had everything working for them: superior weapons and tools, huge populations, the incomparable advantage of written language that enabled them to communicate easily in the present and to transmit knowledge and experience from the past. They had the horse and the wheel. Though some Mexican Indians did have the wheel, it was used only as a toy or ceremonial object, not a tool. White men had centuries of European literature, science, and technology behind them. The Europeans who came to America in its early days brought a great number of skills as well as material equipment. They were highly adaptable and learned to take care of themselves in the wilderness as well as any native. They were also robust, adventurous, determined. There was no stopping them.

Black Hawk and his people might be called the victims of historical inevitability. Once America had been discovered by Europe, the country had to change. Like the effect of a typhoon or an earthquake, such change takes place whether it is desirable or not, and no matter how many Black Hawks go out on the warpath against it.

One more question remains, perhaps the most important of all: Could these inevitable changes have taken place without the wars, the massacres of one race by the other, the tragedies of removal? Were the betrayals, the broken promises, the racial misunderstandings and hatreds unavoidable? Did "progress" and the arrival of the white man demand the Trail of Tears and the Black Hawk War?

What would have happened if the Sac and Fox had been allowed to remain in Illinois, and the Cherokees and Creeks in Georgia and Alabama, and the other tribes more or less in their original homes? The Southern tribes had already made an excellent adaptation to the new facts of American life, and the Sac and Fox probably would have done more farming or worked their lead mines more intensively when the hunting declined. As the large open hunting ranges receded before the advancing line of settlement and industrial development, other tribes might have made similar adjustments. The Indians had already demonstrated their skill and adaptability in taking over many of the white man's materials— the gun, the horse, metal tools and pots—and this was only the beginning. Later, Indians would become successful teachers, lawyers, doctors, skilled technicians and craftsmen in many fields—the Iroquois structural steel workers are an outstanding example—and some would even enter politics, taking part in the white man's government. All they needed was time, time to catch up with new conditions at their own pace and in their own way, and a place where they could live securely, without constant fear of removal.

In 1906, Chief Pleasant Porter of the Creeks told a Senate committee: "It is not so much a question of capacity as it is of time. . . . You are the evolution of thousands of years. . . . Who can say but that we would finally have reached a stage of civilization, toward which we were progressing slowly, but none the less surely, which would have suited our life better than the civilization which has been so violently and suddenly thrust upon us."

There were only a few thousand Sac and Fox involved; there were scarcely one million Indians involved altogether, only a fraction of the millions who flowed into the country from Europe. The Indians had shown themselves willing to sell off large portions of their land, retaining only enough to live on themselves. Today over two hundred million people live in the United States and there has been room for all.

About forty-five years after the Black Hawk War, another Indian warrior, the remarkable Chief Joseph of the Nez Percé in Oregon, led his people in a similar war to save his home. Like Black Hawk he, too, led a famous retreat, struggling through almost twelve hundred miles of difficult wilderness in Idaho and Montana in a futile attempt to reach the safe haven of Canada. Shortly after the war, he wrote:

> I know my race must change. We can not hold our own with the white men as we are. We only ask an even chance to live as other men live. We ask to be recognized as men. We ask that the same law shall work alike on all men. . . .
>
> Let me be a free man—free to travel, free to stop, free to work, free to trade where I choose, free to choose my own teachers, free to follow the religion of my fathers, free to think and talk and act for myself—and I will obey every law, or submit to the penalty.
>
> Whenever the white man treats the Indian as they treat each other, then we shall have no more wars. We shall all be alike . . . with one sky above us and one country around us, and one government for all. For this time the Indian race is waiting and praying.

Note on Spelling

There is great variation in the spelling of tribal names. Europeans, unable to catch the exact sounds of a native language, often mispronounced the names to begin with and then proceeded to spell these mispronunciations in every possible way. Thus Ojibwa became Chippewa, and both these names were sometimes spelled Ojibway and Chippeway. Algonquin has also been Algonkin; Algonkian, Algonquian; and so on. Manhattan appears as Manhattons, Manhates, Manhattanese, among other forms. Wyoming, starting from M'cheuwomink, went through Chiwaumuc, Wiawamic, Wayomic, Waiomink, Woyming, Weyoming, and many other variations before assuming its present form.

Sometimes white explorers, unfamiliar with tribal structure, would name an entire tribe after the name of one of its subdivisions, like a band or clan. When some members of the Meshkwakihug were asked by the French who they were, they replied Fox, which was their particular clan. From then on, the entire tribe was called Fox. Their original name, meaning red-earth people, has also been spelled Muskwakiwuk, Musquakkink, and many other ways.

Sac is just as often spelled Sauk, and at various times in the past has appeared as Sack, Saky, Saukees, Saukies, Sawkeys, Sockeys, Shakies, Saques, Asaukee, Osawkee, and at least a dozen others. The tribe itself used the name Saukies, which is derived from Osakiwug, "people of the yellow earth." I have used Sac, which is the spelling in Black Hawk's *Autobiography* and in the United States military reports and treaties. I have also followed the custom of using the singular form when referring to this or any other tribe as a whole.

Bibliography

In listing the sources for this book, special credit must be given to Donald Jackson's edition of Black Hawk's *Autobiography* and William T. Hagan's indispensable book, *The Sac and Fox Indians*. Virtually all the quotations from Black Hawk are from the *Autobiography,* while Hagan was especially useful for the postwar (Black Hawk War) history of the combined tribes.

Other authors and editors to whom I owe thanks for quotations or for particular incidents taken from their work include Charles Hamilton, Chief Joseph, Angie Debo, Alexis de Tocqueville, James Flexner, Alvin M. Josephy, Jr., D'Arcy McNickle, Carl Sandburg, Albert K. Weinberg, and Jack D.

Forbes. To David Hawke, my appreciation not only for details drawn from his fine book on the colonial period, but for his helpful bibliographical advice and close reading of the galleys. Exact titles of the books and articles of these authors will be found in the bibliography listed below. If I have inadvertently omitted anyone whose name should have been included in this paragraph, I wish to extend my apologies and gratitude, which is deep even though not explicitly defined.

ALDRICH, CHARLES. "Jefferson Davis and Black Hawk," *Midland Monthly,* v. 5 (1896), 406–11.

ANDREWS, L. F. "The Word 'Iowa'—What It Means," *Annals of Iowa,* v. II, no. 6, Third Series (July 1896), 465–69.

ARMSTRONG, PERRY A. *The Sauks and the Black Hawk War.* Springfield, Illinois: H. W. Rokker, 1887.

BAKELESS, JOHN. *The Eyes of Discovery.* Philadelphia: J. B. Lippincott Company, 1950.

BILLINGTON, RAY ALLEN. *Westward Expansion.* New York: The Macmillan Company, 1967.

Black Hawk: An Autobiography. Ed. by Donald Jackson. Urbana: University of Illinois Press, 1964.

"The Black Hawk War," *The Palimpsest,* v. XLIII, no. 2 (February 1962), 65–112. (Articles by Donald Jackson and William J. Petersen.)

BROWN, MARK H. *The Flight of the Nez Perce.* New York: G. P. Putnam's Sons, 1967.

COLE, CYRENUS. *I Am a Man, the Indian Black Hawk.* Iowa City: The State Historical Society of Iowa, 1938.

COLLIER, JOHN. *Indians of the Americas.* New York: The New American Library, 1948.

DEBO, ANGIE. *The Road to Disappearance.* Norman: University of Oklahoma Press, 1941.

DEVOTO, BERNARD. *Across the Wide Missouri*. Boston: Hough-
ton Mifflin Company, 1947.
———. *The Course of Empire*. Boston: Houghton Mifflin
Company, 1952.
DODD, WILLIAM E. *Expansion and Conflict*. Boston: Houghton
Mifflin Company, 1915.
DOWNEY, FAIRFAX. *Indian Wars of the U.S. Army, 1776–1865*.
Garden City, New York: Doubleday & Company, Inc.,
1963.
DRAKE, BENJAMIN. *The Life and Adventures of Black Hawk*. 7th
ed. Cincinnati: H. S. & J. Applegate & Co., 1851.

FAIRCHILD, HOXIE NEALE. *The Noble Savage*. New York:
Columbia University Press, 1928.
FARB, PETER. *Man's Rise to Civilization as Shown by the Indi-
ans of North America from Primeval Times to the Coming
of the Industrial State*. New York: E. P. Dutton & Co., Inc.,
1968.
FEY, HAROLD E., and D'ARCY MCNICKLE. *Indians and Other
Americans: Two Ways of Life Meet*. New York: Harper &
Bros., 1959.
FLEXNER, JAMES THOMAS. *Mohawk Baronet: Sir William John-
son of New York*. New York: Harper & Bros., 1959.
FORBES, JACK D., ed. *The Indian in America's Past*. Englewood
Cliffs, N. J.: Prentice-Hall, Inc., 1964.
FOREMAN, GRANT. *Indian Removal: The Emigration of the Five
Civilized Tribes of Indians*. Norman: University of Okla-
homa Press, 1953.
———. *Indians & Pioneers: The Story of the American South-
west Before 1830*. Revised edition. Norman: University of
Oklahoma Press, 1936.

HAGAN, WILLIAM T. *American Indians*. Chicago: University of
Chicago Press, 1961.
———. *The Sac and Fox Indians*. Norman: University of Okla-
homa Press, 1958.

HALL, JAMES. *Sketches of History, Life, and Manners, in the West.* 2 vols. Philadelphia: Harrison Hall, 1835.

HAMILTON, CHARLES, ed. *Cry of the Thunderbird, The American Indian's Own Story.* New York: The Macmillan Company, 1957.

HAMILTON, HOLMAN. "Zachary Taylor and the Black Hawk War," *Wisconsin Magazine of History,* v. 24 (1941), 305–15.

HAWKE, DAVID. *The Colonial Experience.* Indianapolis: The Bobbs-Merrill Company, 1966.

HODGE, FREDERICK WEBB, ed. *Handbook of American Indians North of Mexico.* 2 vols. New York: Pageant Books, Inc., 1959.

JAMES, MARQUIS. *Andrew Jackson: The Border Captain.* Indianapolis: The Bobbs-Merrill Company, 1933.

———. *Andrew Jackson: Portrait of a President.* Indianapolis: The Bobbs-Merrill Company, 1937.

JOSEPH, CHIEF. "An Indian's View of Indian Affairs," *North American Review,* v. 128 (April 1879), 415–33.

JOSEPHY, ALVIN M., JR. *The Indian Heritage of America.* New York: Alfred A. Knopf, 1968.

———. *The Nez Perce Indians and the Opening of the Northwest.* New Haven: Yale University Press, 1965.

———. *The Patriot Chiefs.* London: Eyre and Spottiswoode, 1961.

LA FARGE, OLIVER. *A Pictorial History of the American Indian.* New York: Crown Publishers, Inc., 1956.

———, ed. *The Changing Indian.* Norman: University of Oklahoma Press, 1942.

"Life of Black Hawk," *North American Review,* v. 40 (1835), 68–87.

LURIE, NANCY OESTRICH. "Indian Cultural Adjustment to European Civilization," *Seventeenth-Century America.*

Ed. by James Morton Smith. Chapel Hill, N.C.: The University of North Carolina Press, 1959, 33–60.

McNICKLE, D'ARCY. "The Indian Tests the Mainstream," *The Nation,* v. 203, no. 9 (September 26, 1966), 275–79.
————. *They Came Here First.* Philadelphia: J. B. Lippincott Company, 1949.
MANYPENNY, GEORGE W. *Our Indian Wards.* Cincinnati: Robert Clark & Co., 1880.
MATHER, INCREASE. *Early History of New England.* Albany: J. Munsell, 1864.
MEESE, WILLIAM A. *The Battle of Campbell's Island.* Upper Mississippi Sketches, 1904.

PARKMAN, FRANCIS. *The Conspiracy of Pontiac.* New York: Collier Books, 1962.
————. *The Discovery of the Great West: La Salle.* New York: Rinehart & Company, Inc., 1956.
————. *A Half-Century of Conflict.* New York: Collier Books, 1962.
PEARCE, ROY HARVEY. *The Savages of America.* Revised edition. Baltimore: The Johns Hopkins Press, 1965.
PORTER, C. FAYNE. *Our Indian Heritage.* Philadelphia: Chilton Books, 1964.

REYNOLDS, JOHN. *The Pioneer History of Illinois.* Chicago: Fergus Printing Company, 1887.
RICHMAN, ROBIN. "Rediscovery of the Red Man," *Life,* v. 63, no. 22 (December 1, 1967), 52–72.

SANDBURG, CARL. *Abraham Lincoln: The Prairie Years.* 2 vols. Vol 1. New York: Harcourt, Brace & Company, 1926.
SCANLON, P. L. "The Military Record of Jefferson Davis in Wisconsin," *Wisconsin Magazine of History,* v. 24 (1940), 174–82.

SCHOOLCRAFT, HENRY R. *Personal Memoirs of a Residence of Thirty Years with the Indian Tribes on the American Frontier.* Philadelphia: Lippincott, Grambo and Co., 1851.

SCHOOR, GENE, with HENRY GILFOND. *The Jim Thorpe Story.* New York: Julian Messner, Inc., 1951.

SNYDER, DR. J. F. "The Burial & Resurrection of Black Hawk," *Journal of the Illinois State Historical Society,* IV (April 1911), 47–56.

STEINER, STAN. *The New Indians.* New York: Harper & Row, 1968.

STEVENS, FRANK E. *The Black Hawk War Including a Review of Black Hawk's Life.* Pub. by the author, Chicago, 1903.

STRODE, HUDSON. *Jefferson Davis, American Patriot, 1808–1861.* New York: Harcourt, Brace and Company, 1955.

THWAITES, REUBEN GOLD. *The Story of the Black Hawk War.* Madison: State Historical Society of Wisconsin, 1892.

TOCQUEVILLE, ALEXIS DE. *Democracy in America.* 2 vols. New York: Alfred A. Knopf, 1945.

TUCKER, GLENN. *Tecumseh: Vision of Glory.* Indianapolis: The Bobbs-Merrill Company, 1956.

UNDERHILL, RUTH MURRAY. *Red Man's America, A History of Indians in the United States.* Chicago: The University of Chicago Press, 1953.

VAN EVERY, DALE. *Ark of Empire.* Boston: Houghton Mifflin Company, 1963.

———. *A Company of Heroes.* Boston: Houghton Mifflin Company, 1962.

———. *Disinherited: The Lost Birthright of the American Indian.* New York: William Morrow & Company, Inc., 1966.

———. *The Final Challenge.* Boston: Houghton Mifflin Company, 1964.

———. *Forth to the Wilderness*. Boston: Houghton Mifflin Company, 1961.

———. *Men of the Western Waters*. Boston: Houghton Mifflin Company, 1956.

WALLACE, ANTHONY F. C. *King of the Delawares: Teedyuscung, 1700–1763*. Philadelphia: University of Pennsylvania Press, 1949.

WARD, JOHN WILLIAM. *Andrew Jackson: Symbol for an Age*. New York: Oxford University Press, 1955.

WASHBURN, WILCOMB E. "The Moral and Legal Justifications for Dispossessing the Indians," *Seventeenth-Century America*. Ed. by James Morton Smith. Chapel Hill: University of North Carolina Press, 1959, 15–32.

———, ed. *The Indian and the White Man*. New York: New York University Press, 1964.

WEINBERG, ALBERT K. *Manifest Destiny: A Study of Nationalist Expansionism in American History*. Gloucester, Mass.: Peter Smith, 1958.

WILSON, EDMUND. *Apologies to the Iroquois*. New York: Farrar, Straus and Cudahy, 1960.

Index

About the Author

Miriam Gurko's interest in the American Indian began with her studies in anthropology at the University of Wisconsin. In Wisconsin she had occasion to see Indians for the first time and to become aware of them as real people, not just romantic figures. She found herself wondering how our history looked from their point of view. This concern was the genesis of INDIAN AMERICA: THE STORY OF THE BLACK HAWK WAR.

Mrs. Gurko has long been absorbed in both history and literature. This interest, combined with extensive training in research, led to her three earlier books: *The Lives and Times of Peter Cooper, Restless Spirit: The Life of Edna St. Vincent Millay,* and *Clarence Darrow.* In them, as in INDIAN AMERICA, her main purpose has been to select representative individuals and present them against the background of their times.

Mrs. Gurko was graduated from the University of Wisconsin, where she majored in history and anthropology. It was there that she met and married her husband, Leo Gurko, who is now a professor of English at Hunter College. She has worked for several magazines and for a publishing house specializing in Americana. While her two children were growing up, she wrote many magazine articles.

Mrs. Gurko was born in Union City, New Jersey, and grew up in Weehawken. She and her husband now divide their time between a New York City apartment overlooking the Hudson River and a country house fifty miles away.

About the Illustrator

Richard Cuffari's paintings have been exhibited in several New York galleries. A number of his illustrations have appeared in the American Institute of Graphic Arts design shows and in the Society of Illustrators annual exhibits.

A native of New York, Mr. Cuffari studied at Pratt Institute. He lives in Brooklyn with his wife and four children.